undergraduate

LELAND STANFORD JUNIOR UNIVERSITY · ORGANIZED 1891

book fund

contributed by
friends of Stanford

THE GREEK TRAGEDY
IN NEW TRANSLATIONS

GENERAL EDITOR William Arrowsmith

AESCHYLUS: **Suppliants**

AESCHYLUS
Suppliants

Translated by
JANET LEMBKE

OXFORD UNIVERSITY PRESS
New York and London
1975

Printed in the United States of America

To Donald Carne-Ross and John Herington

EDITOR'S FOREWORD

The Greek Tragedy in New Translations is based on the conviction that poets like Aeschylus, Sophocles, and Euripides can only be properly rendered by translators who are themselves poets. Scholars may, it is true, produce useful and perceptive versions. But our most urgent present need is for a re-creation of these plays—as though they had been written, freshly and greatly, by masters fully at home in the English of our own times. Unless the translator is a poet, his original is likely to reach us in crippled form: deprived of the power and pertinence it must have if it is to speak to us of what is permanent in the Greek. But poetry is not enough; the translator must obviously know what he is doing, or he is bound to do it badly. Clearly, few contemporary poets possess enough Greek to undertake the complex and formidable task of transplanting a Greek play without also "colonializing" it or stripping it of its deep cultural difference, its remoteness from us. And that means depriving the play of that crucial otherness of Greek experience—a quality no less valuable to us than its closeness. Collaboration between scholar and poet is therefore the essential operating principle of the series. In fortunate cases scholar and poet co-exist; elsewhere we have teamed able poets and scholars in an effort to supply, through affinity and intimate collaboration, the necessary combination of skills.

An effort has been made to provide the general reader or student with first-rate critical introductions, clear expositions of translators' principles, commentary on difficult passages, ample stage directions, and glossaries of mythical and geographical terms encountered in the plays. Our purpose throughout has been to make the reading of the plays as vivid as possible. But our poets have constantly tried to re-member that they were translating *plays*—plays meant to be pro-duced, in language that actors could speak, naturally and with dig-nity. The poetry aims at being *dramatic* poetry and realizing itself in words and actions that are both speakable and playable.

Finally, the reader should perhaps be aware that no pains have been spared in order that the "minor" plays should be translated as carefully and brilliantly as the acknowledged masterpieces. For the Greek Tragedy in New Translations aims to be, in the fullest sense, *new*. If we need vigorous new poetic versions, we also need to see the plays with fresh eyes, to reassess the plays *for ourselves*, in terms of our own needs. This means translations that liberate us from the canons of an earlier age because the translators have recognized, and discovered, in often neglected works, the perceptions and wisdom that make these works ours and necessary to us.

A NOTE ON THE SERIES FORMAT

If only for the illusion of coherence, a series of thirty-three Greek plays requires a consistent format. Different translators, each with his individual voice, cannot possibly develop the sense of a single coherent style for each of the three tragedians; nor even the illusion that, despite their differences, the tragedians share a common set of conventions and a generic, or period, style. But they can at least share a common approach to orthography and a common vocabulary of conventions.

1. *Spelling of Greek Names*

Adherence to the old convention whereby Greek names were first Latinized before being housed in English is gradually disappearing. We are now clearly moving away from Latinization and toward pre-cise transliteration. The break with tradition may be regrettable, but there is much to be said for hearing and seeing Greek names as though they were both *Greek* and *new*, instead of Roman or neo-classical importations. We cannot of course see them as wholly new. For better or worse certain names and myths are too deeply rooted in our literature and thought to be dislodged. To speak of "Helene" and "Hekabe" would be no less pedantic and absurd than to write "Aischylos" or "Platon" or "Thoukydides." There are of course borderline cases. "Jocasta" (as opposed to "Iokaste") is not a major mythical figure in her own right; her familiarity in her Latin form is a function of the fame of Sophocles' play as the tragedy *par excellence*. And as tourists we go to Delphi, not Delphoi. The precisely transliterated form may be pedantically "right," but the pedantry goes against the grain of cultural habit and actual usage.

As a general rule, we have therefore adopted a "mixed" orthography according to the principles suggested above. When a name has been firmly housed in English (admittedly the question of domestication is often moot), the traditional spelling has been kept. Otherwise names have been transliterated. Throughout the series the -os termination of masculine names has been adopted, and Greek diphthongs (as in Iphigeneia) have normally been retained. We cannot expect complete agreement from readers (or from translators, for that matter) about borderline cases. But we want at least to make the operative principle clear: to walk a narrow line between orthographical extremes in the hope of keeping what should not, if possible, be lost; and refreshing, in however tenuous a way, the specific sound and name-boundedness of Greek experience.

2. Stage directions

The ancient manuscripts of the Greek plays do not supply stage directions (though the ancient commentators often provide information relevant to staging, delivery, "blocking," etc.). Hence stage directions must be inferred from words and situations and our knowledge of Greek theatrical conventions. At best this is a ticklish and uncertain procedure. But it is surely preferable that good stage directions should be provided by the translator than that the reader should be left to his own devices in visualizing action, gesture, and spectacle. Obviously the directions supplied should be both spare and defensible. Ancient tragedy was austere and "distanced" by means of masks, which means that the reader must not expect the detailed intimacy ("He shrugs and turns wearily away," "She speaks with deliberate slowness, as though to emphasize the point," etc.) which characterizes stage directions in modern naturalistic drama. Because Greek drama is highly rhetorical and stylized, the translator knows that his words must do the real work of inflection and nuance. Therefore every effort has been made to supply the visual and tonal sense required by a given scene and the reader's (or actor's) putative unfamiliarity with the ancient conventions.

3. Numbering of lines

For the convenience of the reader who may wish to check the English against the Greek text or vice versa, the lines have been numbered according to both the Greek text and the translation. The lines of the English translation have been numbered in multiples of ten, and these numbers have been set in the right-hand margin. The (inclusive) Greek numeration will be found bracketed at the top of the page. The reader will doubtless note that in many plays the English lines outnumber the Greek, but he should not therefore conclude that the translator has been unduly prolix. In most cases the reason is simply that the translator has adopted the free-flowing norms of modern Anglo-American prosody, with its brief, breath- and emphasis-determined lines, and its habit of indicating cadence and caesuras by line length and setting rather than by conventional punctuation. Other translators have preferred four-beat or five-beat lines, and in these cases Greek and English numerations will tend to converge.

4. Notes and Glossary

In addition to the Introduction, each play has been supplemented by Notes (identified by the line numbers of the translation) and a Glossary. The Notes are meant to supply information which the translators deem important to the interpretation of a passage; they also afford the translator an opportunity to justify what he has done. The Glossary is intended to spare the reader the trouble of going elsewhere to look up mythical or geographical terms. The entries are not meant to be comprehensive; when a fuller explanation is needed, it will be found in the Notes.

ABOUT THE TRANSLATION

With the possible exception of *The Persians*, no extant Greek play presents the translator with a severer challenge than Aeschylus' *Suppliants*. Like *Prometheus Bound*, it is the sole survivor of a trilogy, but its dramatic action is visibly less complete, as its meaning is darker, more teasing and uncertain. In its range, running from high religious lyrics to scenes of grim, almost farcical, melodrama, it is formidable indeed; it also has an overwhelmingly choral quality, that aura of "archaic oratorio" that once led scholars, wrongly, to call it the "oldest surviving Greek play." Worse, even if the poet succeeds in scaling this translator's Everest, his work is unlikely for obvious reasons ever to be staged; and his achievement will be recognized for what it is only by scholars—by those, that is, who know that this tough, ticklish, and beautiful fragment is, in its own way, even more taxing and perilous than the high rigors of the *Agamemnon* or *The Trojan Women*.

A play like this requires not only good Greek but quite extraordinary resourcefulness in the poet; the translator who sticks too closely to the literal Greek is lost before he starts. Here freedom is not merely useful but absolutely necessary. Freedom, but also the talent to use freedom well—freedom trained and willing to take responsible imaginative risks. Janet Lembke is not, by academic standards, a professional Hellenist; she is, as her own poetry and this translation make quite clear, a remarkable poet who happens to have remarkably good Greek. Too little Greek is crippling; too much, as Nietzsche knew, can intimidate its possessor, inhibiting risk and talent alike; what counts is having, as in Mrs. Lembke's case, good enough Greek to recognize linguistic necessity, and therefore, poetic opportunity; to know when risk is required and when there is simply no alternative to spirited freedom.

Mrs. Lembke took her undergraduate degree in Classics at Middlebury College; she is presently a part-time graduate student in Greek at Boston University. Her poetry and translations have been widely published in such journals as *Arion*, *Poetry Northwest*, and *Contemporary Literature in Translation*. In 1973 she published that distinctive anthology entitled *Bronze and Iron: Old Latin Poetry from Its Beginnings to 100 B.C.* (University of California Press), an extremely impressive effort, both poetically and critically, to recover, from its dormant and fragmentary life, the texture of religious experience in archaic Latin poetry. She is now working on a translation of Pindar, and also studying oral and ethnic poetry, traditional and contemporary, in America.

In his own self-composed epitaph, Aeschylus made no mention of his poetry and dramatic career; he preferred to be remembered simply as a soldier "who fought the long-haired Mede." With similar modesty and conviction, Mrs. Lembke insists that poetry and literature are not her "essential occupation." She is, as she simply and quite undefensively says, a housewife; she has a husband and four children. *E basta*. Why, after all, should she apologize? Housewifery, no less than soldiering, is a way of life which brings one bone-close to birth, love, and death, which are the absolutes of poetry. The sensitive reader will recognize that Janet Lembke's Eleusinian feeling for life, her reverence for the sacredness that shines in ordinary things, for the fresh-seen textures of the old and archaic, her intuitive leap from the fragment to the whole, have been honed against her own life, against good hard domestic truth.

Her Greek has acquired its cutting edge on tougher demands than classroom drill. And her perceptions have been sharpened on harder questions than graduate students are trained to ask. She has acquired, and kept, her Latin and Greek under conditions that would make even hard-working university teachers blench. She returned to the study of Latin and Greek (if she ever left it), not, I suppose, as a drug against domestic work, but because she felt in it the affinity and pressure of an old *daimon*—something that both revealed and was revealed by common daily life. Now, to a play which retells part of the primal myth of human marriage, she brings a familial mind and a married imagination; she invests the tale of Io, the maiden-turned-heifer, with her own childhood on a farm, a life of "real moos and bawls . . . clanking stanchions . . . the fusty sweet warm snuffling dark of a cowbarn at night." To the most archaic of Greek plays, she brings an old pagan sense of divinity, won, by observation and hard work, from good words and good life reciprocally shaping each other.

Lincoln, Vermont   WILLIAM ARROWSMITH

CONTENTS

SUPPLIANTS

INTRODUCTION

I

Aeschylus' *Suppliants* is a stepchild in the house of surviving Greek tragedy: a beautiful but intractable bundle of contradictions that have prompted perplexity and argument. The play has therefore been tucked away and put to work in academic chimneycorners. It has admirers among scholars, yes, but few students of drama, fewer everyday readers encounter it. It deserves better.

Yet, it is not an easy play. The many lyrics have been acclaimed, justly, as the loveliest of all tragic lyrics, but an eighteenth-century translator described the play as "fraught with fine poetry and pious sentiment, but on the whole a drama devoid of nice art in its construction and a tragedy without a tragical conclusion." Then, the play's language is opulent, but the stage action implied by the words —no stage directions ever accompanied the play proper—seems so meager that some modern critics have thought of *Suppliants* as an oratorio rather than a theater piece. The feelings expressed by the lyrics are profoundly religious, but the myths informing them are fabulous, exotic, cruel, and repellent.

The play's construction also presents problems. It has been termed archaic and even primitive. Choral odes are uniquely predominant, commanding more than half the present text. The story seems to call not for the classic twelve-member chorus but for a stage-filling crowd of fifty suppliant women, each with an attendant maid. No one knows how many Suppliants actually appeared on stage, but however large the Chorus, its role is that of a single protagonist.

For these and other purely internal reasons of structure and style, *Suppliants* was long believed to be truly archaic, a not quite classical work that reached pastward to tragedy's lost antecedents for its form. And it was long thought to be the oldest tragedy extant, composed and presented perhaps as early as 490 B.C. It would thus have preceded *Persians* (472) by almost two decades and the *Oresteia* (458) by more than thirty years. The play seemed, therefore, the work of a young poet whose skills and dramatic imagination were still green. Recent evidence, however, supports a date in the last decade of Aeschylus' seventy years. *Persians* now lays fair claim to seniority.

That evidence merits a few words, for its discovery is an example of the kind of miracle scholars pray for but are seldom granted. In Egypt, appropriately, a papyrus fragment was found. Its publication in 1952 struck classicists with the force of Zeus' customary weapon, for it bears external information on *Suppliants'* date. It declares, in a widely accepted reconstruction of time-eroded words, that a tetralogy by Aeschylus—the tragic trilogy of which *Suppliants* is the first member and a concluding satyr-drama, *Amymone*—took first prize in a dramatic competition and defeated a group of plays by Sophocles. And the fragment mentions the name of the archon then presiding in Athens. The dates for these magistrates are established. *Suppliants'* production is thus placed no earlier than 466 and most likely in 463.*

This new information in no way explained the play's unusual features. It provoked instead a host of prickly questions. Was the play a bit of juvenilia pulled out of storage? If so, why was it produced decades after it was written? If not, its archaism must have been intentional. Why then did the mature poet reach deep into the past for his form? Barring future miracles, there may never be an end to argument.

Nor is the conflict between internal archaism and late date the only source of argument. Many of the play's tensions are obvious: male-female, barbarian-Hellene, private interest-public welfare, chastity-marriage, and fantasy-reality. But the play's fifth-century implications can only be guessed at. Did it celebrate the establishment of a women's festival or support women's rights? Did it comment obliquely on Athens' relations with Egypt and Argos? The play's theme is also elusive. Is it the inscrutability of Zeus' mind that in its perfect stillness moves to order the universe? Is it the clash between manmade law and the laws of heaven? Is it perhaps a cautionary defense of marriage? Opinions bristle; nothing is proved. The present text is corrupt, and attempts at interpretation are made triply diffi-

---

* *Oxyrhynchus Papyri*, xx (1952), 2256, fr. 3. For a thorough discussion of its possible reconstructions and interpretations, I am indebted to A. F. Garvie, *Aeschylus'* Supplices: *Play and Trilogy* (Cambridge University Press, 1969), pp. 1-28.

cult by the loss of the two plays, *Egyptians* and *Danaids*, that followed *Suppliants* and brought its story to a conclusion. It is as if *Agamemnon*—an *Agamemnon* robbed by time of its climactic murder—were all that survived of the *Orestcia*. Agreement exists only on these points: *Suppliants'* lyrics are numinous, and its substance almost as inscrutable as Zeus.

But the scholars' arguments do identify the questions that challenge any new translation. Is the play tragic? (Are there tints and shades of tragedy, fractions of tragedy?) Then, what is the play about? And, are the play's peculiarities dictated by dramatic necessity? Ancient Greeks, like Delphic oracles, are not available for consultation. The answers found must be answers that work here and now without slighting the play's antique strangeness.

II

Suppliants' physical plot is uncomplicated. The story takes place in the prehistoric Greek past. The scenc is set near the city of Argos. The orchestra, where the Chorus enters and dances while singing the odes, represents a shore. The raised stage behind the orchestra is a sanctuary crowded with images of gods—Zeus, Apollo, Poseidon, Hermes—and one altar common to them all. Enter the Danaids, the fifty virgin daughters of Danaos. Each carries a fresh-cut branch, the traditional symbol of suppliance. In Greek custom the suppliant petitioned from a shrine or sanctuary for asylum. At the moment of taking up the branch its bearer came under the jealous protection of the gods. Zeus, above all others, was thought to be the special guardian of those who sought asylum. In this role he was invoked as Zeus Suppliant. The epithet defines his protective function; there is no implication that the god himself was a suppliant. If asylum was granted to the petitioner, it was held to be a god-enforced, inviolable right.

The Suppliants immediately make it known that they are terrified fugitives from the land of Nile. They have fled marriage to their violently lustful cousins, the fifty sons of their father's brother Aigyptos (Egypt). At this very moment the would-be bridegrooms are swarming in swift-sailed pursuit. In a long choral ode (50-201) the Suppliants give thanks for safe arrival in Argos and express fear that their troubles are not yet ended. At the ode's conclusion their father enters and cautions them to take refuge in the sanctuary. Urging them to be calm, he warns that an explanation of their presence in Argos will soon be called for by the armed delegation now approaching. On its arrival the maidens ask the leader, Pelasgos king of Argos, to receive them as suppliants and they claim ancestral ties to his country. The petition presents Pelasgos with a choice of evils. If sanctuary is refused, the gods, offended by such sacrilege, will surely punish Argos. But if the Suppliants are sheltered, war with Egypt is a certainty, for the Egyptians do seem to have a valid legal claim upon the women. In either event the Argive people will suffer. The king's indecision and anguish are clear, but he is given direction by the Suppliants' threat to hang themselves from the images of the gods. And he agrees to put the case before the citizens, whose vote by Argive law must be final arbiter. He sends Danaos into the city to put branches on the temple altars and thus make the presence of suppliants known to the populace. After promising to speak to the people on their behalf, he too departs. The Danaids, now alone on the shore, sing and pray. As they deliver their most heartfelt praise of Zeus the Allfather, their own father re-enters with the glad news that the citizens' vote was affirmative. While the Danaids bless the Argive land and people in another ode (861-942), he climbs to the sanctuary, a vantage point from which he soon sights the Egyptian ships. Though he tries to reassure his daughters by saying that it takes time to moor a fleet, they are terrified. But, telling them that the gods protect them, Danaos leaves to muster help. The women's fears are not unjustified. Before help arrives, an Egyptian herald and a troop of armed men come ashore. The herald orders the Suppliants shipward. When words fail to move them, he uses force. But in the nick of time Pelasgos enters with soldiers. The herald makes war-talk but departs. Pelasgos asks the Suppliants to let him escort them to the city, but when they refuse to leave the sanctuary without their father, he too departs. Danaos soon returns with an honor guard of spearmen. And, to the singing of a recessional ode (1345-1422), *exeunt omnes* to the city.

But that is merely the play's immediate action. There is a super-plot that takes place in the remote past. Throughout the play, the Suppliants sing the story of the princess Io, their four-times-great grandmother, whose Argive birth reinforces their claim to asylum. Io, keeper of the keys to Hera's temple, attracted the attention of Zeus and was transformed by the ever-jealous goddess into a cow guarded by Argos, the thousand-eyed watchman. But Hera's precautions did not avail. Hermes slew Argos, and Zeus, lusting still, turned himself into an amorous bull. Hera again attempted to put an end to her consort's dalliance by sending a gadfly to torment Io. To escape its merciless stinging Io fled from the very shore on which the Suppliants stand. Maddened by pain, she swam the sea and galloped over Asia until, circling southward, she came to the land of Nile, where she fell exhausted in a meadow sacred to Zeus. There he again visited her and restored her to human form by breathing upon her and touching her. By his divine breath and touch alone she conceived and bore a son, Epaphos, whose name means touch or caress. The Suppliants see Io's sufferings as parallel to theirs, and they hope for a release as gentle as hers. At play's end it seems that this hope may be realized, for Argos has accepted and promised to defend them.

Plot and superplot are linked by more than apparently parallel action. There is an interweaving of rich thematic images. Over and again the Io-cow and the Zeus-bull are evoked in other contexts. The Suppliants see themselves as a driven herd and compare their plight to that of a lost heifer harried by wolves. They pray for the fertility of Argive herds and sing of pastures and refer to brideprices paid in cattle by the Egyptians. The touch of Zeus also rests on the play. His palm, his caress, his unbruising fist are hymned in continuing counterpoint to the seizure by rough hands that the Suppliants fear. His breath, too, blows changefully throughout as breeze and wind and hurricane. And Hera's gadfly achieves hideous new life in the "manswarm," the "wingèd horde," of Egyptians.

Other recurrent images serve to give the play integrity. Its air is filled with the rush of wings: hawks, a nightingale, carrion crows, vultures. The Suppliants cry out in "birdvoices," pain nowhere shows "the selfsame feather," and the very gaze of Zeus becomes a bird, alighting on rooftops and staining them as it perches. The play's earth is endlessly fertile: flowers, fruit, grasses, grain. The verbs of procreation are those used specifically for planting and sowing. The Egyptians are sprouts on an old vine, Danaos compares his daughters to succulent summerfruit, and Zeus "plants the lifepulse in green nature." And Earth's dust is constantly refreshed by sweet water: Nile, Io's fathering river, Argos' rivers that curl redgold toward the sunset, and its sun-oiled streams.

But where is tragedy? Though interlocking themes and pervasive imagery give the play a coherence of its own, it is not truly self-supporting. The plot finds no ultimate resolution. Little is known about the two lost plays, but mythographers have recounted the Danaid legend often enough so that we have a few of the details that must have shaped subsequent action, though they may not have been shown directly on stage. In their light *Suppliants* appears to be the prelude to tragedy.

The Egyptians did come, conquer, and claim their brides. On the wedding night, at Danaos' behest, all but one of the bridegrooms were stabbed to death. (The surviving couple, Hypermestra and Lynkeus, began a line notable for Zeus-luring daughters: Danaë, mother of Perseus who was conceived in the god's golden rain, and Alkmēnē on whom he fathered Herakles by assuming her husband's shape. But neither of these beguiling ladies takes part in the Danaids' story.)

Careful opinion holds that a trial figured in the trilogy's development. Murder was, of course, a polluting offense against men and gods. But so were vow-breaking and filial disobedience on the part of the daughter who swore to kill but spared her husband. It was apparently she who was tried and found innocent. It seems, too, that Aphrodite intervened on her behalf. A magnificent seven-line fragment from the trilogy's last play is logically given to the goddess. It celebrates sexual love and its object, reproduction, by praising the divine marriage of Earth and Sky. That wedding, sacred and fruitful, provides the cosmic model for mankind. And it must not be questioned.

No one knows what fate, if any, Aeschylus visited upon the murdering daughters. Legend says that they did eventually marry and that after their deaths they were eternally condemned to the task of carrying water in sieved jars. These late events are not at all likely to have figured in the trilogy.

Amymone, the lost satyr-play that followed the trilogy's performance, seems to have concerned itself with a lighter episode in the Danaids' lives. Danaos sent his daughters, Amymone among them, to find water. The quest appeared to be futile, for Poseidon, angry at Argos, had at that time dried every known spring, river, and pond. As the Danaids searched, Amymone threw a dart at a deer and struck a satyr, who immediately assaulted her. As she attempted to fend off his shaggy advances, Poseidon appeared, routed the satyr, and promptly thereafter carried out the satyr's lustful intentions on his own behalf. In fee he revealed to Amymone an unfailing source of water, the spring at Lerna.

III

Though the Greeks saw *Suppliants* as tragic in the context of its trilogy and said as much when they awarded Aeschylus first prize, it is not enough to accept their judgment. We cannot see the play as they did. The music, dances, and masks are irretrievably lost, and the ambience of performance. Only the verbifact endures, and it is no longer perfect. If the play is ever again to be perceived as more than a curiosity, it must by itself move emotions here and now. If it is to find new dramatic vigor, the one surviving element, the broken text, must contain an intrinsic something that withstands time travel and culture shock: a psychological plot that links its antiquity to our present moment. I have reread *Suppliants* as presenting a particular account of a timeless human occasion, an occasion that recurs constantly and is not itself changed—however much human responses to it do vary and change—by shifts in landscape, religion, law, customs, language, and notions of what drama and poetry are.

Enter the Suppliants, not fifty but twelve. They are drenched to the knees because they have just waded ashore from a boat. They are black because Nile's sun has looked upon them, and they are comely—bodies as curved and tempting as fruit ready to be picked, faces reflecting the fierce independence of desert nomads, clothes glittering with barbarous splendor, breasts bare. They are virgins of an age to marry. How old is that? Their father addresses them as children and girls, but they speak of themselves, and the king addresses them, as women. And indeed they are women fullgrown, the youngest provocatively nubile, the eldest middle-aged, perhaps greying, but still full of female juices. They are ripe and overripe for husbands and children.

But they will NOT marry (12-13):

Agree to marry Egypt's sons   unthinkable!
skin shudders   the unholy thought

Later, in a chilling lament (1027-98), they cry that they would rather be taken by death than forced to wed. And why not marry, when marriage is expected of all women? The reason given is that Egypt's sons are violent and marriage would give them license for repeated sexual brutality. Again and again the Suppliants mention Egyptian *hybris*, a word that signifies an arrogance that blinds its possessor to the might of the gods and makes him aspire to more than human status. In fifth-century Athens *hybris* was also a technical legal term meaning "rape." In the context of *Suppliants* it has been translated as "lust." For a reason to be given later, I think it cannot be simply "rape" or "lust," though it bears those emanations when it is applied to the Egyptians. I have instead translated it with various compounds using the key syllable "self-"—self-vaunting, self-serving, self-blindness, self-glory, self-love.

The Suppliants' desperation is extreme. Rather than marry Egypt's sons, who are in fact brutal and motivated by selfish lust, they have chosen secret flight. And when they appeal to the king for protection, they make it plain that if their god-honored suppliance is refused, they will choose a god- and man-shocking form of suicide—hanging themselves from the images of the gods. It is as if, in another day, they had threatened so to use a crucifix or the tablets of the holy ark.

At first the refusal to marry and the threat sound like the polemics of a women's liberation movement, the Suppliants raising their branches like fists clenched for self-determination. But no, it is soon clear that they expect the course of their collective life to be determined by others—their father, the king, the gods. And they have used past events, the Io-history, as predictions of their future. So often have they called to mind Io's agony and deliverance that they have come to think of it as their own experience not yet fully lived out. What was, shall be. They feel, they *know* that they, too, deserve to be gently freed from their trials. In justification of their refusal to marry they often cite *dikē*, the basic principle of natural order and rightness, the laws of heaven. They *know* that divine law sanctions their behavior. In the play's moment, however, they are panicky refugees who cannot read how far into the future their trials will last.

I read their beliefs as false. The Suppliants have mistaken terrified hope for preordination. They do little to save themselves but pray and threaten and curse, sometimes hysterically, while they wait for touch and breath. Their very panic, however, suggests that they do sense something amiss. They are, after all, suppliants begging for sanctuary in the name of Zeus and requesting human help, force if necessary, against the pursuing Egyptians. And until help shall come from gods and men, they defend themselves with a shield of fantasy, a dream of deliverance absolutely promised, that blocks their recognition of plain facts: time is irreversible, no one goes home.

The Suppliants' psychological predicament may be read, here and now, as a primeval variation of the Beauty and the Beast story. In its classic resolution the virgin Beauty at last leaves her father's house and accepts the Beast for the goodness of spirit concealed within his grotesque body and thereby also accepts, according to modern interpreters, the forever-joined contradictions that exist in all life: evil-goodness, ugliness-grace, animal urge-human will. She thus attains true womanhood and finds her own humanity of spirit. But the Suppliants' story is unresolved. Though in body they are grown women, they steadfastly reject the Egyptian "Beasts" and continue to live, archetypal victims of a father fixation, in their father's house. The play, moreover, asks an important question about the identity of that father. Is he the physical, human father Danaos? Or is he Zeus the Father, who as Io's lover was male parent of the Suppliants' line? The play begins with an invocation to Zeus "Father Protector" and soon turns to the Suppliants' "father on earth, heart's guide and guide for our footsteps" (14-15). By play's last third the word "father" is used twice in an ambiguous vocative that can refer to either one (1081 and 1173). At play's end the two are inextricably confused, and there are strong suggestions that the Suppliants harbor an unrecognized incestuous desire. If their release from suffering is truly to parallel Io's, this desire is insanely reasonable.

But the play deals with matters larger than problems of the female psyche. Marriage is not the critical issue. Nor are the Suppliants motivated by anything as narrow as fear of Egyptian brutality or a personal aversion to cousin-marriage, which Greek law permitted and sometimes mandated in the statutes declaring that fatherless daughters were bound to marry their next-of-kin. A father could so pledge his daughters before his death. Nor were the Suppliants driven, as has been surmised, by an inborn pathological loathing of all men or an inability to come to terms with their own sexuality. The rejection of marriage and the women's stubborn, childish, father-abetted fantasy are the play's metaphors for a refusal to assume adulthood. That refusal is, I believe, the cornerstone of the play's psychological plot. Of course, it is not a play just about women. Its specifics point to the general occasion that links its world with ours. The occasion is coming of age. And coming of age certainly means more than learning to live with sexuality. It means making a contract with one's society, even if the contract is sometimes sealed with a resounding NO. It means reaching voluntarily and hopefully toward the unknowable future and trying to shape it. It has meant (till very recent attempts to limit population on a large scale) a millennia-long commitment to assure human survival through the birth of new generations. It still means putting away the child's way of thinking that confounds metaphor with literal meaning and sees the childself as the center of the universe. Two resolutions are possible for the Suppliants: death or love. In the play's own terms: an insanely murderous defense of childishness or growing up. And here, surely, is tragedy—deeprooted and impossible desire set against inexorable biological, social, and psychological necessity.

And what of Io, both Beauty and the Beast in one person? She and Zeus himself are invisible actors in the psychodrama, and it is their impalpable presences that enlarge the play by giving it a past and infusing its mortal moment with eternity. But Io's history that so encompasses and permeates the play should be a dreadful warning to her granddaughters. Until mid-play she is described flatly as girl or cow or mother. She is a person or animal referred to, remote and fabulous. Then, the Suppliants sing her story from beginning to end (684-813), and in the singing Io-sung appears. It is as if she is actually present, a figure as real as the Suppliants themselves. Fly-stung, stampeded, she "hurls her body down Asia toward unreachable sunrise." Valleys fall behind her, mountains rise in her footsteps as her mad flight transforms a continent. She is an

undreamed apparition
   grasseater, flyblown
patchflesh halfhuman
There
     and there
          she is cow
and here
     still woman lowing and marvelous

The people who see her are appalled; their hearts skip beats, they cannot help staring. Her shape is woman's but she is horned and patches of hair disfigure her skin like angry new grafts and her hands are hoofs, she must lie on the ground to feed. Hers is no natural cowness but the sign of an inward horror. There is a monstrously egocentric child inhabiting her mind and heart; it breaks through, begins to consume her. And she cannot be transfigured till she—*she*, not a god—releases that childself and turns futureward, a woman whole, full of the breath of life and touched by faith, hope, and confidence.

Her story is that of the Suppliants resolved on a divine level, the gentle, momentary fusion of mortal flesh and immortal spirit. The Suppliants believe, however, that Io remained virginal throughout her love affair. Or rather, they try not to disbelieve; they firmly reject Pelasgos' suggestions that Io and Zeus were entangled in the usual manner of man and woman and that their son's conception was something less than virginal. But their most secret feelings about that ancestral coupling slip out when they refer to it in words overtly reserved for the Egyptians: "force" and "seizure." The Suppliants nevertheless fail consistently, tragically, to read the lesson in Io's metamorphoses: that to persist in childishness is to become less than human.

And what of the Egyptians, Io's four-times-great grandsons? They appear like dogs, like spiders and vipers in a black dream out of Egypt. The women have fled them not so much because virginity is imperiled, marriage repugnant, and Egypt's sons violently lustful, but because the sons are also Io's children, the darkside of her moon. Whatever true legal claims they have to the Suppliants, their animal-like desires surely defy the laws of nature and natural order. Nor can they control the forces of humanity and bestiality that war within them. They are threatened by the same end—to lose all human qualities, to become animals irretrievably—that awaits the Suppliants should they persist in their flight, which is a flight not merely from marriage beds but from the demanding realities of life. Again, the Suppliants seem to sense the potential for wrong in their attitude. They resist the Egyptians, and that resistance is a last-ditch survival tactic, a gut reaction, to protect their own humanity. But marry the Egyptians, marry them not, the women are ironically doomed by their own *hybris*. The word they hurl at the Egyptians turns on them. Self-vaunting self-glory, self-righteous self-interest are their own blinding characteristics. They are damned unless they, like Io, can perform an act of self-transfiguration.

What is the nature of these women? The usual view has been that they are sweet, amiable, plaintive, modest, brimming with filial piety; that they personify virtue as the Egyptians personify evil. Vaporous Victorian maidens? Hardly. They are passionate, they are fierce, they tremble with barely suppressed sexual appetites. Their language is the language of thwarted fertility; it teems with genital symbols—flowers, rivers. Two of their many odes contain elaborate curses, one directed against Pelasgos (535-64), the other against the Egyptians (1120-68). Two odes are laments (50-201 and 1027-98), though, as they admit in the former:

> . . . rites for the dead
>   in fair times when death is a stranger
> surge godward bearing a bloodcurse

They are as amiable as streams in spate, as innocent as murder. It is no wonder that Pelasgos, the model of reason, cannot easily decide to welcome them, however much he first admires what he thinks is the dauntless courage that brought them to his shore. The confrontation between Suppliants and king unfolds like a trial (426-517); they are at once petitioners and prosecutors, and he, somehow defendant and unwilling judge. At play's beginning the Suppliants are already spinning down into madness and dehumanization, a fate that is slowly made clear in piling references to defilement, murder, and death. In the opening lines of the play they protest their innocence, "Leaving it [Egypt] we flew, not outlaws hounded publicly for murder's blood on our hands, but fugitives. . . ." The protestation is an oracle: there shall be blood and death.

Yet the Suppliants are to be pitied. Though they have not understood their plight, their hope for deliverance and their fear are heartbreakingly real. Their prayers are heartfelt. Transfiguration is indeed imperative, but circumstances have not yet presented an appropriate means of release. Marriage is destiny in the Suppliants' world; not to marry is a violation of *dikē*. The Suppliants are caught in a dilemma. And, menaced by crude and loathsome cousins, they are at the mercy of strangers. Their father, "heart's guide," does in every way prompt their ultimately murderous intransigence.

Danaos' role in *Suppliants* has puzzled many critics. His part, in contrast to that of Pelasgos, has seemed naïvely written, and his presence nearly superfluous except when he assumes duties usually assigned to the tragic chorus, which the Chorus here cannot perform, taking as it does an actor's part. As quasi-chorus Danaos advises and chides and reports the offstage action—the citizens' affirmative vote, the arrival of the Egyptian fleet—that further stage action. (It is suggestive, though probably not significant, that in this two-actor tragedy the actor who played Danaos also took the Egyptian herald's role.) Danaos has most often been seen as a kindly old soul motivated by nothing other than genuine paternal concern for his daughters' wellbeing. How can such a man be father to insanity? How indeed?

I see him enter not when he first speaks (202) but when he is first mentioned (14). Bent and ancient, he comes in silence, mounts the place of gods, and assumes a silhouetted attitude of prayer. In his shadow-stillness it is as if he is become a god, listening. Soon he hears his daughters tell the eerie story of a woman changed into a nightingale and kept from rest in her "green leafrivers." As she flies, hawk-pursued, she sings her home- and heartsickness, and (76-79)

. . . the notes spill old tears with new
   as she sings her son's doom:
he was killed and she by her
own hand's anger unmothered

The Suppliants are most obviously comparing the nightingale's flight and grief-song with their own; in the next verse they say, "My human voice is also sorrow's friend." But what extraordinary, what monstrous prophecy! However unwittingly, the women have also compared themselves to a murderess, a filicide. After this play's end they shall at their father's command kill the Egyptians and kill as well a chance to bear children. They shall sever themselves from the life-continuum. And at the moment of singing the murderess they must feel in a deep, unacknowledged corner of their souls that their father is also killing their own capacity to act as godly human beings. At one point Danaos even seems to identify himself with Zeus; he speaks of his own gazing eye (946) with the Greek word used elsewhere for deity's vigilant gaze (476, 877-8, 1046). The play has a madman, and it is Danaos, author of his daughters' lives and their plight and their deepening insanity. He, more than the Egyptians, is villain. He, too, is Io's son.

His absolute power over his daughters is made clear from the play's beginning. And as the play unfolds, it is his counsel that repeatedly urges them to reject society's expectations and to suppress their quite natural sexual stirrings. Even after it seems that the women, accepted as refugees, will be saved from forced marriage to the Egyptians, he admonishes them saying, in a final speech that borders on the salacious, that they are like succulent summerfruit and that their voluptuousness will inevitably entice men. "Do not shame me," he warns. "Guard a father's commandments; love your chastity more than your lives." He will not have them marry anyone. Why not?

The play does not offer reasons that will satisfy a modern audience. But myth does, and an ancient audience might well have known them, though such knowledge would not necessarily have enhanced fifth-century appreciation of the trilogy. The myth appears in many conflicting versions, but one detail common to them all is that Danaos quarreled with his brother Egypt. Some versions give an immediate sequel to the quarrel: Egypt suggested reconciliation and as proof of good faith offered his sons as husbands for Danaos' daughters; when Danaos refused the suit, Egypt vowed to kill him and his daughters. In that vow alone there is motive enough for the flight from Egypt. Danaos has cause to fear the Egyptians as much as the Suppliants do, for his own skin is at stake. Several versions also add that before Danaos left the land of Nile, an oracle had told him that his son-in-law would kill him. Thus, while there is only one threat to his daughters' lives, Danaos is twice-menaced, by his brother's known hand and the hand of a nameless son-in-law. To save himself he encourages his daughters' tragic dependence and drives them to a lunatic fear of marriage and sexuality. Later, the mass marriage accomplished, it is his command that thrusts the knives into Egyptian hearts.

Pelasgos' role counterpoints that of Danaos. The two have been seen as playing somewhat similar parts, that of the Protector and that of the Parent. But as Egyptian maleness and force are antithetical to the Suppliants' femininity and weakness, so Pelasgos and Danaos represent opposites. There is an obvious black and white difference in appearance; Danaos comments (652): "Nile and Io's fathering river, each nurtures its own race." And their characters are as dissimilar as their skins. Pelasgos looks outward to law and reason for solutions to the problems presented by the Suppliants; Danaos consults inner experience. Pelasgos acts out of consistent concern for the public good; Danaos, out of self-interest. Granted that the Suppliants' world is a patriarchal one in which women were usually subject to men's wishes, still Pelasgos makes suggestions to them and solicits their understanding; Danaos dictates. Pelasgos stands on the side of peace and life; Danaos brings with him an unbreakable promise of war and death.

But at play's end not one drop of blood has been spilt. In the concluding ode (1345-1422) ambiguous notes are sounded, portending grief to come. The Suppliants, leaving for their new home, laud the country and its gods in a recessional literally overflowing with sexual imagery:

> No more shall we sing hymns to quell Nile
> spilling its siltflood into the sea

Sing praise to rivers that rise here
  and thrust through homefields
the sun-oiled streams
    that here shed their pleasurous waters
    to sweeten the dust of the mother Earth
  and fulfill her with life upon life

In the very next breath, however, madness cries to Artemis, goddess of chastity, "Help us withstand the womb's need for fullness that opens virgins to Aphrodite's act."

They are immediately rebuked. The next lyrics have been given by one scholar, at least, to the honor guard of spearmen accompanying Danaos; most critics believe, however, that they are to be assigned to a sub-chorus of Egyptian ladies-in-waiting who came ashore with the Suppliants and now, after a thousand lines of silence, burst into song. The words do seem most appropriately spoken by women. And I think that it is more dramatically effective, here and now, to put them in the mouths of Argive women, brought from the city by Danaos to attend his daughters. These servants are not able to accept the Suppliants' repudiation of woman's proper social role:

But Aphrodite is not slighted here
  nor do her rites lack eager celebrants . . .
And she is thanked, guile-dazzling
  goddess, for her solemn games.

And the Suppliants are warned that they may claim no special grace from heaven. They answer with a cry to Zeus that he deliver them as he delivered Io, though they are ready to admit that the final triumph they ask for may not be entirely favorable to them. But partial victory is better than none at all: "Better the half-light than utter dark." They have in their own minds behaved with guiltless obedience to heaven's laws; they are certain in their fantasy that they must be rewarded with heaven's benevolent attention.

To us who have not learned our myths in the cradle, the play falls on its back, not on its feet. We have been prepared for storms, but nothing happens. The actors depart, the play is over. The psychological tensions—forecast horrors, slowly piled thunderheads of coming violence—linger undissipated. Members of the antique audience would have known full well that darkness would almost totally eclipse the Suppliants. But, unacquainted with the story and hampered by the loss of the plays that swept the trilogy to its end, we are left unsatisfied with an empty stage.

From the second play, *Egyptians*, one word of Dionysiac ecstasy is left. From the third, *Danaids*, there survive two solidly attested fragments, a three-line excerpt referring to wedding customs and the earlier-mentioned benediction spoken in praise of marriage and fertility. Scholarly research has also assigned several one-line fragments to *Danaids*, and a few Aeschylean lines not attributed to specific plays seem as if they could have been fatherly maxims spoken by Danaos. I have combined all of these into a postlude that carries the Suppliants to their storm's end; it will be found in the Translator's Notes following the play proper.

IV

There are no hard facts of literary history to account for *Suppliants'* structural peculiarities, such as the preponderance of lyrics and the Chorus as protagonist. But if the text is read as an account of an occasion, coming of age, that has been immemorially ritualized, like the occasions of child-naming and marrying and dying, then the drama may play out in imagination like a rite of passage. Procession of ode and episode, the structure suggests the solemn public patterns of liturgy, patterns meant in themselves to evoke a sense of the sacred, patterns that seem to echo the lost rituals of a strictly choral type of pre-tragedy. Introit through recessional to the last lovely benediction sung by the goddess, the play's real drama is as invisible as transubstantiation. It should enact itself within players-audience-lone reader like a gale, like a god's breath, buffeting everyone with ritually worked changes of feeling, great leaps from hope to sorrow and terror to hope again.

It is not of course a rite. It never was. Rite deals with the desire for continuity in human life; tragedy with breaks in the relationships between men and men, men and their gods. But *Suppliants* can be seen as a piece of ritual theater that combines the patterned emotional transformations of rite with a kinetic visual experience, no matter that the experience may now be one solely for mind's eye. No oratorio or cantata this, with only the choir's lips moving. The lyrics are immensely pictorial; images—birds, cattle, the sea, ships, rivers, mountains, breezes, and tempests—flash swift and kaleidoscopic through the imagination. And the singers become their songs, they dance the nightingale and her flight, they are Io. They grow larger than their physical selves to become all girls on the threshold of maturity.

Suppliants' ritual aspect seems inherent. If so, it would help to account for the apparently archaic form into which Aeschylus cast a well-known myth. And the words I use to re-create it are words that I hope will speak to whatever is left of a modern sense of the ceremonial and the sacred and so make the play's antique strangeness somehow familiar and bring its timeless emotions home.

V

This translation is, admittedly, a sometimes radical reappropriation of *Suppliants'* one surviving element, the Greek text. Its aims are three and equal. The first is homage. For the sake of verbal access to the play Aeschylus' images and metaphors are translated with fidelity. Cattle graze, rivers stream, and Zeus holds the scales. I have strived for some reproduction of Aeschylus' remarkable compound words, verbal balances, and even syntactic distortions where they point up poetic and dramatic ambiguities. The plot, of course, unfolds just as it does in the Greek. The second aim is that of making the play emotionally accessible. Aeschylus' irreproducible meters must yield to the English and circadian rhythms that seem affective equivalents. Dead allusions are replaced by phrases meant to evoke felt responses here and now. When there is conflict between literal accuracy and what I believe is an accuracy of feeling, the latter prevails. Lexical readings, however, are given their due in the notes, which are keyed to the numbering of the English lines. The third aim is playability. *Suppliants* was composed to be danced and sung and spoken. It should still have a chance for oral publication, either in the speech of players or a silent voice in the mind's ear of a reader.

Readers will notice that the English version is many lines longer than the Greek. The disparity is more apparent than real. Much of it is accounted for by the fact that I have often translated one long Greek line as two, sometimes three, short English lines. And some of it stems from explanation; a concept expressed by a word or two of Greek may need fuller treatment to be understood by today's reader.

Throughout, the only rule has been, Trust the poet. If Aeschylus implies that Zeus' gaze is a bird, then the gaze is not *like* bird but *is* bird. And he knows that man, to be man, bleeds and dies but never is there blood on divine hands. I have tried most of all to preserve, in ways intelligible to a secular time, the ancient sense of awe, pity, and terror that pulses in the lines.

The translation is based on the texts of H. Weir Smyth, *Aeschy-*

lus, volume I, Loeb Classical Library, Harvard University Press, 1922, and of H. Friis Johansen, *Aeschylus: The Suppliants*, volume I, København, 1970. Where the texts differ, I have freely followed the version that seems to me more effective. My choice and its reasons appear each time in the notes. There will be those who feel I have taken monstrous liberties in translating feelings rather than words, and to them, if they are Greekless, I commend the sober and faithful prose readings accompanying both texts *en face*. Or better still, the study of Greek.

Many other books have been helpful in bringing *Suppliants* to life in my mind. Three must be individually acknowledged: A. F. Garvie's *Aeschylus' Supplices: Play and Trilogy* (Cambridge University Press, 1969); Robert Duff Murray's *The Motif of Io in Aeschylus' Suppliants* (Princeton University Press, 1958); and Margaret Alexiou's *The Ritual Dirge in Greek Tradition* (Cambridge University Press, 1974).

And people—most important are the people who have continually encouraged me, offered scholarly criticism, pulled the reins when my fancies flew headlong, and just plain listened. James Hynd, of the University of Texas, deserves great thanks for tape-recording *Suppliants* so that I could hear the Greek ryhthms. William Arrowsmith gave needed polish, especially in matters theological, to my understanding of fifth-century thought. And there are two who have been extraordinary partisans from the beginning. Words enough to thank them do not exist. To Donald Carne-Ross and John Herington, therefore, this version is dedicated.

Westport, Connecticut   JANET LEMBKE
October, 1974

SUPPLIANTS

CHARACTERS

SUPPLIANTS
DANAOS their father
PELASGOS king of Argos
SPOKESMAN a son of Egypt
CHORUS of Egyptians
CHORUS of Argive women
Argive soldiers and spearmen

Line numbers in the right-hand margin refer to the English translation only, and the Notes at p. 79 are keyed to these lines. The bracketed line numbers in the running headlines refer to the Greek text. Lines bracketed in the translation are reconstructions, based on context, of Greek lines that are now corrupt or completely lost.

An Argive shore with a raised sanctuary where the gods offer asylum. Grouped around a common altar, images of Zeus, Apollo, Poseidon with trident, and Hermes.

Enter the SUPPLIANTS from the left. Each carries the emblem of suppliance, a branch wreathed with white wool.

SUPPLIANTS ZEUS MEN APHIKTOR Shining Father
        Protector of suppliants   shine freely
here   on this voyage of women   who set sail
where Nile twists through saltpolished
sand   Hallowed netherland whose sunbruised
boundaries graze desert   leaving it
we flew
        not outlaws hounded publicly
for murder's blood on our hands
                but fugitives   10
escaping self-built prisons for our own flesh
Agree to marry Egypt's sons   unthinkable!
skin shudders   the unholy thought

          DANAOS enters left and climbs to the sanctuary.

Our father on earth   heart's guide
and guide for our footsteps   gambling
all for the best among sorrows
            decided
we fly before we were pinioned   over a trembling sea
to light on this earth cupped in the day's hand
and here   it must have been   our lives,   20
our voyage time out of mind began in
    droning of flies round a heifer
    warm palm of heaven
    blue breathing of Zeus   yes
we swear it!

Land? shall you welcome
our coming?
With these mightiest swords we implore you   with
branches flowering white unspun wool

O home   30
O earth and sundazzled water
Highblazing gods and slowgrinding earthpowers
            vital in coffins
O Saviour Zeus
            guarding the flesh houses
of men who honor You   receive as Your suppliants
our fleet of innocence   and breathe
a soft air of mercy onshore

                                    But the night-thick
manswarm   self-vaunting, spawned out of Egypt   40
before one foot pierces the shallows
before sailwings fold   God!
send them seaward   breathe rain, ice and winter
caress them with lightning, thunder, hail
let them face gnashing waves
                                    let them die
before they can man themselves   decency forbid!
in cousin-beds, in bodies seized and
      brutally entered

    Putting down their branches, the SUPPLIANTS *sing and dance.*

O be joyful now sing   50
      the Zeus-calf born over the sea
         to right an old wrong
son of our flowerpastured first mother
child of the heifer filled by Zeus' breath
caress-child whose name,
      given at birth, proves the virginal
      truth of his fathering:
Epaphos, Caress-born

Sing joy sing homecoming!
   These green shores nourished   60
     our earliest mother
   while her body learned the first stings of suffering
   Remember her pains   count and recount them,
   proofs of our good faith
     proofs to astonish the land's children
   till they know truth
abides in our unfinished story

If a diviner of birdsong comes near
   a landsman who hears our heartfelt lamenting
he will think that he listens   70
   to her who was wife and now
sings out heart's darkness,
a hawk-shadowed nightingale

Barred from her nest in the green leafrivers
   she trills strange sweetness lamenting her exile
and the notes spill old tears with new
   as she sings her son's doom:
he was killed and she by her
own hand's anger unmothered

                                   80
And singing Io's song
my human voice is also sorrow's friend
Mourning fingers rake smooth cheeks
   Nile's endless summer burnt
Tears corrode a heart unused to tears
I pick grief's flowers in the shadow of fear
   Are there friends here?   Or kin?
   For us who fled that land wide as air
   who will here lament and bury us?

But gods who gave me life
O hear me, stand vigil over heaven's laws   90
Grant innocence no wedding night
   that thrusts against fate

Self-serving lust!   Welcome it with hate
that saves me rightfully from wedded rape
   Even the battle-weary who run
   find an altar, a sword-free no-man's land,
   within their fearful love of heaven's powers

And Zeus!   grant that my hopes all come true
   But Zeus' desire is not easily traced
   for the paths of His mind   100
   maze through dusk and briers
   and my eyes cannot follow

It falls surefooted, not on its back,
   whatever command Zeus shakes from His head
   And it flares in the dark
   and carries black portents
   that men cannot read

And He hurls men down from hope's
heaven-tempting towers   their bodies
lie broken   But He needs no force   110
to complete His armor

   Out of that pure center where He sits throned
   unmoving He moves
   and His will has been done

Let Him look down and behold brute
self-seeking   how green the old
vine grows   new sprouts shooting forth
to entwine us in marriage
answering their untrainable hungers

   They run drunk and wild, goaded by lust   120
   And mad loins breed
   a madness in their minds

Disasters of pain
   I tell them in funeral cadences

keening, griefheavy, tearstormed
alalala
      lamentations
My voice is the wail of all funerals
I live I chant my own deathsong

      Lighten me   healing Hillpastures   130
      My cry holds Egypt's savagery but
      Mother-earth   you know my voice
        I try I try with mourner's hands
        to tear the fine-spun veil
        that shrouds my sight

But rites for the dead
   in fair times when death is a stranger
surge godward bearing a bloodcurse
ulululu
        pain unfathomed   140
Where will its waves wash me?   where break?

      Lighten me   healing Hillpastures
      My cry holds Egypt's savagery but
      Mother-earth   you know my voice
        I try I try with mourner's hands
    to tear the fine-spun veil
        that shrouds my sight

Broad oars, yes, and a house of planks
   bound with cord stitches to keep out the salt
brought me homeward unstormed on wind's steady breath   150
   Nor do I complain

But my heart thinks of death
Father Allvisioning
   grant it lifegrace again

      If only the seeds
        of a godembraced mother

might fly from men's beds
    away away away
    unmated, unraped away

See me!   stainless daughter of Zeus   160
  safekeeper of gates to your maiden shrine
I would guard my chastity as you guard yours
  but I am pursued

With your hunter's strength
as virgin for virgin
  save me from touching man

    If only the seeds
      of a godembraced mother
    might fly from men's beds
      away away away   170
    unmated, unraped away

If not, black flowers
forged by Nile's beating sun
shall seek
  that earthen hostelry
  where the Zeus rich in guests
  finds room for the lifeweary
and shall knock with suppliant branches
and enter noose-hung into death
    unless the gods on the skysummits hear us   180

    Zeus!   revenge against Io
    collects endless payment
    O I know Your queen's
    heavendaunting envy
      A day of hard wind
      blows a night of storm

And if I die
shall a just indictment not

trap Zeus:
>   that He has disavowed   190
>   the heifer's child, the son
>   He fathered long ago
because He turns His countenance
away from supplicating prayers?
>   But God in the highest   NOW hear our crying

>   Zeus!   revenge against Io
>   collects endless payment
>   O I know Your queen's
>   heavendaunting envy
>   A day of hard wind   200
>   blows a night of storm

DANAOS Children!   be cautious.
Caution disembarked you here, and trust
in the elder wisdom of your captain-father.
Standing now on firm ground,
looking futureward, I warn you.
Guard the words, carve them on memory,
for I see
>   dust, voiceless messenger
of an army on the march.   210

But its wheels are not silent,
they squeal round the axles.
A mass of troops, yes,
shieldenclosed and spearbristling,
I see the shapes,
the horses, the curved chariots.

We are the likely cause:
this country's leaders
would confirm with eyes
what ears have learned from messengers.   220
But be it harmlessly or be it
sharpened by raw anger

that this march is risen toward us,
it better suits all frames of temper
that you sit, sheltered in your innocence,
upon this rock where gods are met.
Stronger than any fortress, an altar;
no mere man can breach its shield.

Quickly, quickly, rise, climb,
your whitecrowned emblems   230
that especially delight Zeus' pity
held solemn in the hands of luck—
those on your heart's side.

The SUPPLIANTS *pick up their branches. Some move toward*
                                    the sanctuary, some linger.

In sorrowing, respectful, modest,
and most needful voices
you shall answer the strange host
as befits an uninvited guest.
Tell them plainly of your flight:
it was not murderstained.
And let birdvoices hold no brash notes.   240
No doubts must furrow
the smooth brow of your self-control,
no flirtation gleam in virtue's eyes,
and no forereaching, no backdragging
rule your words, for either breeds
a swift opposition in these men.

Remember, bend!
You are in want, strangers, fugitives,
and rash tongues do not suit
the part of weakness.   250

A SUPPLIANT   Father, yes,
              your caution speaks to mine.
              Memory shall guard the treasure of your words.
              But Zeus!   First Father, SEE US!

DANAOS May His eye hold you tenderly.
Don't loiter now. Borrow strength from purpose.

A SUPPLIANT From you, I want to stay near you.
O God, this weariness, have pity.
Shall I never be free?

The last SUPPLIANT *reaches sanctuary.*

DANAOS *moves from image to image. As he identifies each
one, the* SUPPLIANTS *severally lay branches at the base.*

DANAOS Zeus does as He wishes. Praise Him.   260

A SUPPLIANT Praise takes wing, flies toward the sun.

DANAOS And Apollo, god who spent a year on earth.

A SUPPLIANT Who knows, then, about human troubles.

DANAOS Knowing them, he may defend you.

A SUPPLIANT Will other powers here fight for us?

DANAOS This trident is a god's weapon.

A SUPPLIANT Poseidon's waves were kind to us.

DANAOS And one more, Hermes, honored in Greek custom.

A SUPPLIANT Let him herald our freedom!

The SUPPLIANTS *sit at the feet of the images.*

DANAOS All heregathered are your lords.   270
Praise them with trembling.
Settle in their cleanness,
a pitying of doves who know hawkfear:

wingèd kin for hating,
blood cousins desecrating their own kind.
Bird that feeds on bird, how is it clean?
And one who preys upon a girl
against her will, and mine,
can he be cleansed?
                              Never!   280
Even after death there is no flight for him:
he shall be charged for an unnatural act,
and wrong shall be avenged.
Rumor says there is another Zeus
who sits in Hades and chars
final vengeance into all who have
worn out their earthly lives.

Remember:
guard your eyes, speak softly, bend!
Be sure of victory.   290

                    PELASGOS *enters right with his soldiers.*

PELASGOS Where
              have you come from?   A congregation
glittering, bizarre in alien robes and diadems,
and womanly, yet gaudy as no women
I have ever known or dreamed.
And how
              have you come here?   Without forewarning
or invitation.   Helped and guided
only by a reckless courage.   I am amazed.
But the branches   300
              that lie beside you in godshadow
seem lawhonored signs that you claim asylum.
At this one point perhaps your world meets mine.

Conjecture can solve every riddle.
What answers will your voices bring?

32

A SUPPLIANT   My clothes, my branch:
              your observations are not-false.
              But whom do I answer?   Private citizen,
              spokesman, priest or holy prophet?
              Or the people's leader?   310

PELASGOS   Reply to me, speak directly in good faith to me.
              For I am Pelasgos,
                  sprung from the seed of this Ancient Ground
              that grew in Earth's womb.   I rule this realm.
              And I
                  for these good reasons stand first
              among the land's many sons who harvest
                  her deep sweetness.
              Over plains, over valleys
                  where rivers curl redgold   320
              toward the sunset, I hold all power.
              Beyond eyes' north horizon
                  to mountains that build immense palisades
              against the wild tribes,
                  to foothills where oaktrees
              rustle their oracles,
                  until sea restrains me
              with its bluesalt marches, I hold all power.
              And the region around us
                  has been called immemorially   330
              Bull's Pasture in thankful memory of a healer.
              Apis, God's Bull, was his name,
                  and he sailed here,
              a hero with healing visions, Apollo's own son.
              And he cured our fields of mansavaging predators,
              cleared our houses of the choking dragoncoils
              that sick Earth, drenched,
                  infected by the bloody stains
              of ancient murders, had spawned in agony.
              With such finecutting, freeing surgery   340
              did he excise her pain that Argos still pays
              his reproachless name a fee of prayer.

You have my credentials now.
Claim your lineage and corroborate it
quickly.

　　My home has never cherished empty speech.

A SUPPLIANT My history is brief and plain. Argos
　　　　　cradled me.

　　　　　　　　I claim it proudly as birthright
　　　　　through a childblessed cow. All this is true!   350
　　　　　I offer proof: a few more words.

PELASGOS Strangers spin me incredible tales. How
　　　　　can Argive soil and air be yours by birth?
　　　　　Women seeded in the fields of Libya, surely you
　　　　　resemble them rather than our native daughters.
　　　　　And Nile might nurture such luxuriance.
　　　　　And, Cypriot craftsmen do stamp male conceits
　　　　　of female forms like yours on copper blanks.
　　　　　And like you the nomads I hear of, sunburnished
　　　　　women who saddle their humpbacked horses,   360
　　　　　the camels, and ride Ethiopia's borders.
　　　　　And, the husbandless, fleshfeasting Amazons—
　　　　　if you bore weapons, certainly you would be they.

　　　　　But tell me more. Perhaps I may then understand
　　　　　how birth and heritage make Argos yours.

A SUPPLIANT A keeper of the keys to Hera's house,
　　　　　the girl Io,

　　　　　　　　do people say she lived in Argos?

PELASGOS They say it and believe it.

A SUPPLIANT And say that Zeus Himself desired her?   370

PELASGOS No secret from Hera that deflowering.

A SUPPLIANT Outrageous! What did she do?

34

PELASGOS A cow, our goddess turned girl into cow.

A SUPPLIANT Did Zeus go near the horned cow?

PELASGOS They say He took bull's form and covered her.

A SUPPLIANT So they say. What did Zeus' bedmate do next?

PELASGOS She set a thousand eyes to guard the cow.

A SUPPLIANT An allseeing herdsman for one cow. Who?

PELASGOS Argos, son of Earth. Hermes killed him.

A SUPPLIANT Did she do something else to the unlucky cow?   380

PELASGOS She sent a cattlegoad, biting, bloodsucking—

A SUPPLIANT A fly, Nile's people say a blowfly.

PELASGOS —that drove her from land when she tried to outrun it—

A SUPPLIANT Yes, our stories interlock!

PELASGOS —but she found lower Nile and the city of sphinxes.

A SUPPLIANT Yes! God's hand caressed her and planted His seed.

PELASGOS Who is the cow's Zeus-calf?

A SUPPLIANT Epaphos, named for the true way Zeus took His prize.

[PELASGOS And his child?]

A SUPPLIANT Libya, great and fertile.   390

[PELASGOS And her bounty?]

[A SUPPLIANT Agenor was her firstborn.]

PELASGOS Had she another offshoot?

A SUPPLIANT Baal, father of two sons and one MY father.

PELASGOS Now tell me his respected name.

A SUPPLIANT Danaos, whose potent brother has fifty sons.

PELASGOS His name? Don't hold it back.

A SUPPLIANT EGYPT!
Now you know how ancient blood flows new in me.
I beg you, act. Raise me from this holy refuge.   400
TAKE ME HOME!

PELASGOS You seem to inherit true communion with my country,
and out of the deepest past. But, familiar houses,
how had you courage to abandon them?
    What rush of fortune swept you here?

A SUPPLIANT Pelasgos, lord of my people,
human sufferings change color in a flash; pain
never lets one glimpse the selfsame feather.
Who wished unexpected flight? foresaw that terror
would impel your kin by ancient marriages to cower here,   410
refugees, hating the thought of bridal beds?

PELASGOS Explain more clearly why you stand suppliant before the gods.

A SUPPLIANT Not to be enslaved by Egypt's brood!

PELASGOS Because you hate them? Or have they violated laws?

A SUPPLIANT What woman would marry a slavemaster?

PELASGOS But marriage means clan-strength and man's increase.

A SUPPLIANT If marriage fails, divorce is easy.

PELASGOS How is a godfearing man supposed to help you?

A SUPPLIANT Never give me to Egypt's sons, no matter what they claim.

PELASGOS You ask me to bear the burden of a new war.   420

A SUPPLIANT But heaven's law protects its human allies.

PELASGOS Yes, *if* that law was always party to the case.

> *The* SUPPLIANTS *rise and hold their branches over the images.*

A SUPPLIANT I crown your state's helmsmen. Respect them!

PELASGOS My skin crawls when I see my gods overshadowed.

A SUPPLIANT No man can bear the burden of Zeus Suppliant's wrath.

SUPPLIANTS Son of this Ancient Ground, let kindness
    hear me   Lord of my people, let heart's vision
    see me
        a suppliant, a refugee running here, there
    wolfharried   430
          a calf trapped on a mountain ledge
    trusting her life to the rockshield, bawling again
      again to the herdsman
    Fear   Weariness   Save me

PELASGOS I can see,
    beneath new-cut branches, shadowy
newcomers thronging the presence of my gods.
I wish it harmfree,
    this right that strange guests claim to our houses.
Or shall it bring to pass,   440
    uninvited by my people, unforestallable,
a bloodfeud, the visitant no people welcome?

SUPPLIANTS   Bear witness, Suppliant Themis, daughter
             of Zeus Jury-Appointer: my flight harms no one.
             And you
                         lord full ripe in wisdom, learn from the later-sown
             Human cries
                         for heaven's help and man's are due respect
             and when the altar shields a suppliant, then
                 you, a king, must show the gods   450
                     fear   trembling   obedience

PELASGOS   But you do not sit
                 as claimants to the safety of my private hearth.
             It is the body politic, the people,
                 that may be contaminated;
             in concert they who must then cure their houses
                 and their lives of bloodghosts.
             And I, one man, can offer you no contract
             until the citizens, all of them,
                 publicly debate your case.   460

SUPPLIANTS   You   the people!   You   the government!
             A pharaoh chosen, unimpeachable   you
             sustain the fire blazing on the country's altarhearth
                 with single-voiced decrees, your own,
             and single-handed from your sovereign bench   you
             bring all debts to final reckoning
                     Beware heaven's curse

PELASGOS   Heaven's curse—
                 may it fester only in my enemies. But you—
             I cannot war on your behalf without incurring damages   470
             nor yet, lightheartedly, dishonor your petition.
             I am made weaponless.
                 Fear beats in my body like a pulse:
             to act, or not to act and let chance deliver
                 its blind verdict.

SUPPLIANTS   His gaze is vigilant   O lift your eyes
             to Him Who guards all trial-torn humanity

Shall one who sits before her own kind pleading heaven's law
    find no relief mandated
in the laws of men?   Zeus Suppliant's anger   480
burns unquenchable though its victim
    lament to the end

PELASGOS If—hear me!—

    if power over you is vested in Egypt's sons
by the law you were born to, because they are
your nearest kin, who would contest it willingly?
It is compulsory—do you hear me?—
    that your defense spring from the law you fled:
that therein they have no jurisdiction,
    none whatever, over you.   490

SUPPLIANTS Never
    not ever
    may the power of a male fist crush me
    With help instead from sailorguiding stars
    I chart my own course   flight
    from a loathsome marriage

    As your ally now choose heaven's law
        Decide!
           Offer loving fear to the gods

PELASGOS There is no facile judgment for the case.   500
    Choose not me as judge.
I have told you, tell you now, not without
    the polity's consent
may I act on the question, not even though I rule,
    lest in time to come,
if anything in any way untoward should happen,
    the householders convict me:
Aliens. When you honored them, you damned your people.

SUPPLIANTS We share
    one blood and   510
    spring from one vigilant God Whose hands

weighing human differences fairly dispense
vengeance to the profane
blessings to the reverent

    Heaven finds balance but you scruple
        Why?
            Earthly justice is yours to achieve

PELASGOS There is need—see it!—
        for deep and saving counsel,
just as a diver descending the fathoms needs   520
a clear eye undazed by the sea's winy rapture.
Counsel, so that foremost your suit bring
        no hurt to my people,
and counsel, for my own sake, that it be
        settled peacefully
and no force roughly seize its prize,
nor may we surrender you while you sit
        before the court of gods
lest Zeus Alldestroyer break holy,
heavy into our houses and we bring upon ourselves   530
        His ceaseless vengeance
that even after death lets no man go free.

    Consider! Can you not see now
        the need for counsel that saves us all?

SUPPLIANTS Be counseled   and become
        it is your   allredeeming right
our dutiful heavenwary
advocate
        The refugee   do not betray her
farflung and cast upon this shore   the waif   540
        unholy lustfulness pursues

    Nor witness me   from the seat
        of a godhost   roughly prized
reclaimed like a thing stolen
O you in whom

                              rests ALL power   from sea to mountains
Wake now to the self-adoration   of Egypt
      Beware an eversearching wrath

Nor bear   to watch idly as one sanctuaried
      is forced from the godstones   550
          though asylum is my heavensent right
and dragged off
      a wild colt
                    my crownband
the halter   my hair, fine rope   and strange
      hands pawing my flesh

And know   to your children and their generations
      it shall be given
          whichever groundwork you now lay for them
to pay Doom   560
      full tribute in
                              death or
rejoicing   Reflect   How just the power
      downstreaming from Zeus

PELASGOS Doubt not,
          I have reflected,
          and thought grounds here:

          harsh war
          in one cause or the other
          and I must fight: 570

          last nail driven home,
          the ship held in winches
          strains toward the sea:

          but there shall be no landfall free from pain.

          If treasures have been looted from a house,
          then may Wealthguarding Zeus [in jealous charity
              make good the loss,]

and if a tongue shoot words that hurt,
then may speech enchant speech back to wholesomeness
   [or twist the arrow in the wound.]   580

But that there come no murder of blood kin

I must
offer sacrifices,
victims must fall:

the gods
in their multitude demand
a multitude as ruin's cure.

Your animosity
repels and pulls me in
though I have wished   590

for ignorance,
not knowledge,
of a killing night:

and still I hope
against all reasonable hope
for peace, for light.

A SUPPLIANT Pity me. And listen to my final argument.

PELASGOS Argue on. I shall hear every word.

A SUPPLIANT I have a breastband and ribbons to fasten my dress.

PELASGOS Things common, no doubt, to women everywhere.   600

> One SUPPLIANT *removes her breastband and collects two
> others. Handing the ends to another* SUPPLIANT, *she begins
> to make a braid.*

A SUPPLIANT Now out of them—look closely—an eloquent device.

PELASGOS Singing tongues, rhythmic hands. Put words to your music.

A SUPPLIANT If you can make us no firm promise—

PELASGOS Cat's-cradle. What purpose in your game?

A SUPPLIANT New strange offerings to give the godstones splendor.

PELASGOS A riddle for an answer. Speak plainly.

The finished braid is knotted into a noose.

A SUPPLIANT To hang myself, and now, AND FROM THESE VERY
GODS!

PELASGOS Your words are whips that flay my heart.

A SUPPLIANT You understand! Now I have made your mind's eye wake.

PELASGOS Yes.   610

And the truth is as hard to grapple as a river.
Evils in surfeit crest sudden, sweeping me down
to an unchartable sea of tears and death. The depths
open, and nowhere a port safe from evils.

If I do not discharge the debt
owed you in heaven's name,
your sworn befouling of both gods and men
shall never be outshot.

But if I stand, back to the wall, and battletest
the issue with your cousins, Egypt's sons,   620
shall not the cost be bitter: men drenching
trampled earth with blood, and all in the name of women?

Yet, that any of us live, I must
revere the lethal holiness of Zeus,

for He is Stay of suppliants,
and mortal flesh owes Him its highest fear.

(*to* DANAOS)
And you,
   respected father of unmarried daughters,
bundle their branches quickly in crooked arms,
   take them   630
to other altars of my country's guardian powers,
 and lay them down,
   tokens for the eyes of all men
that you have come in suppliance.
   Otherwise their tongues
will send a spate of arguments against me,
for people here enjoy disputing leadership.
But,
   if the sight of branches stirs their pity,
then shall they despise a male armada's selfishness,   640
then shall my countrymen grant you their welcome.
All men recognize some sympathy for helplessness.

DANAOS It is worth much to us, understanding
   that a godmoved voice will plead a stranger's cause.
   But, companions, guides with native knowledge of the land,
   send them with me to the altars of the tutelary gods,
     those city-guarding crocodiles that slumber
     in the lifestream of your nation,
   so that I find the temples easily, walk the streets
   in safety: 650
     my dress, my face are not like yours.
   Nile and Io's fathering river, each nurtures its own race.
   Beware: overconfidence gives birth to fear,
   and men have cut down friends they did not recognize.

PELASGOS (*to his soldiers*)   Men in the first rank, march with him.
   The stranger our guest speaks persuasively.
   Guide him to the city's altars, where gods abide,
   and when you meet others, no need to be garrulous

about this voyager you steer to safety
  at the firesides of gods.   660

> DANAOS *takes some of the branches and exits right with a*
> *detachment of soldiers.*

A SUPPLIANT You instructed him and he has gone.
But I? What am I to do?

PELASGOS Come. Leave your branches there.

A SUPPLIANT Yes, I'll leave them as you ask.

> *The* SUPPLIANTS *place the remaining branches on the altar.*

PELASGOS Here, below the altar's rock, you may exercise.

A SUPPLIANT Unconsecrated public ground! How can it keep me safe?

PELASGOS We shall not give you to the wingèd horde.

A SUPPLIANT They are more poisonous than snakes!

PELASGOS I speak to you reasonably. Reply in kind.

A SUPPLIANT But they frighten me.   670

PELASGOS You have nothing to fear.

A SUPPLIANT Then encourage me by what you say and do.

PELASGOS Not long, not long shall you be left fatherless.
And I—
    there are people to be called from fields and hills.
I, too, must go
    to soften them toward accepting you with friendship
and tell your father how to please their ears.

Wait here. There are gods
   in the earth, on the heights, in this air.   680
Hymn them. Pray that your desire be fulfilled.
I shall do as much as one brief man can do.
May persuasion guide me, and good fortune follow.

PELASGOS *waits until the* SUPPLIANTS *descend and exits right*
                                         with his soldiers.

SUPPLIANTS Lord over lords   of the everblest
Most Blest   of prayer's answers
Answer Perfected
               Zeus God
    Whose wealth is the earth and the heavens
let prayer now win You
From Your own daughters   690
ward off the manpride that stalks us
    Hate it with splendor
Down seadeeps grave it
                    Sea's blue night
will heal over slashing black oars

Look now on women   look kindness
upon us   whose line reaches back
to the longfabled past
             to her
    who began it, the woman You cherished   700
Renew within us
her glad deliverance
Court memory, how gently Your
    palm caressed Io our mother
Zeus Father
         WE ARE YOUR DAUGHTERS
and hers who was forced from this home

As the SUPPLIANTS *sing Io's story, they dance it in spectacu-*
lar pantomime. Through them Io becomes an overwhelm-
             ing, though unseen, presence on the stage.

Ancient days, ancient footprints
   I move now among them
My mother flowerbrowsing,   710
sleeplessly watched,
   here foraged on spring grasses and from here
flystung, stampeded,
mindbroken she runs

Many many the nations of men
     She has transgressed them
      Sea sunders land from land
    To the east, helpless, doomstormed
   she tears a dry wake through the windblasted water
till she marks solid ground,   720

hurls her body down Asia
   toward unreachable sunrise
Sheepgrazing solitudes,
straight through them she drives
   to the teeming squares and alleys of towns
And she tramples valleys,
mountains rise in her footsteps

Many many the faces of earth
    She has transformed them
     Forever swift rivers well   730
   in her track, her rush harrows stone,
  unburies the earthquake, the speed of her flight
scythes grain in the fields

And now she arrives
   body plundered by bites
   of the whinywinged drover
at the green oasis holy to Zeus
where all creatures may pasture
   on snowsuckled grasses
where quick showers strike   740
and air

thickens
　　　　to rainsmoke
and here
　　　　to Nile's incorruptible water
demented she comes　　　her anguish unearned
mindsick and bodysick　　　goaded
tormented　　　a shebeast
　　infected and holy

And the people whose lives   750
　　the rich land sustains,
　　　corpsegreen their horrorstruck faces
Hearts skip beats, eyes cannot stop staring:
undreamed apparition
　　grasseater, flyblown
patchflesh halfhuman
There
　　　　and there
　　　　　　she is cow
and here   760
　　　　still woman lowing and marvelous
And now in extremity　　　who shall transfigure her
body and mind　　　wretched
farharried　　　flycursed
　　and burdened with horns?

Who lives without end
　　King of gods and men
Zeus . . .
In the fist of unbruising power
In the radiant storm of His breath   770
she found rest
　　tears fell
　　　washed away
　　　　all grief and disfigurement
Zeus-filled she conceived
　　　　　　　IT IS NOT FALSE!
and bore Him a son immune to reproach

who lived a life
   crowned with years and gold
All lands under heaven rejoice with singing   780
Zeus Who plants the lifepulse in green nature
surely quickened this child and his children
Who else
   could arrest
     a goddess-born
      mortal infection?
Zeus alone, and we
        IT IS TRUE!
are daughters born to His hand's Caress

               DANAOS *enters right.*

On earth a godhost gives   790
   order to nature
     Which god shall I cry to?
     Whose acts will answer me?
The Father
   Urge of my green life
   Whose own hand has sown me
Lord
   Ancient in wisdom Who crafted my people
   Allhelp
   Whose fair breath has sped me   800
Zeus

In high fiery places He sits
   suppliant to no throne
     nor derives His might
     from a more potent king
No other
   enforces His homage
   nor is He valley overshadowed by summits
But He
   acts in the instant of speech   810
 · His word

has completed whatever His will
conceives

O Father Lord Zeus no other but He conceives Father

The SUPPLIANTS *chant and rechant the last words until*
they are hysterical.

DANAOS   Calm yourselves, children.
And be joyful.
The citizens play their part well.
In the assembly all-enabling measures have been passed.

A SUPPLIANT   Elder statesman!
You bring the news most hoped for.   820
Tell me, tell me,
what decision has been made? Where
did the hands of the majority
show winning strength?

DANAOS   The men of Argos voted not ambivalently
but so that my old veins ran hot and young again.
In full assembly every man raised his right hand—
air bristled!—to confirm this resolution:

THAT WE BECOME SETTLERS IN OUR MOTHERLAND,
FREE, SECURE IN OUR PERSONS   830
AGAINST ALL SEIZURE AND HUMAN REPRISAL;
THAT NO MAN, EITHER NATIVEBORN OR ALIEN,
DRIVE US OUT INTO CAPTIVITY,
BUT, IF FORCE BE EXERCISED,
HE WHO DOES NOT AID US,
THOUGH IT IS HIS RIGHT AND DUTY TO BEAR ARMS,
SHALL LOSE ALL RIGHTS,
HIS EXILE MANDATED BY HIS PEERS.

And with what style did he prevail on our behalf,
Pelasgos lord of the Argive people,   840

50

speaking of Zeus Suppliant's wrath and its immensity;
warning that never in all time to come must people fodder it;
and saying that if we, doubly guests and kinsmen,
should cause a double mist of blood to shroud the people,
it would breed past human cure the fatted beast of ruin.

Hearing this, hands high,
not waiting for the usual reading,
the assembly voted:
LET IT BE LAW.
O they were easily persuaded,   850
listening to the twists of rhetoric.

But it was Zeus Who sealed the resolution.

He climbs to the sanctuary and stands looking left toward
the sea.

A SUPPLIANT Come sisters
come sing for the people of Argos
blessings of thanks in return for their blessings

And Zeus Guest and Stranger!
keep watch over strangers
that the prayers on our tongues come true
that now and tomorrow
no one reproaches them   860

HALFCHORUS Now   O gods
      OF created of God   hear us now
SUPPLIANTS We overflow with prayers for our people

Never may they know the peace
that scorched earth brings
nor hear the famished glee
of carnal Ares
who harvests flesh
where men have sown their seed

For they pitied us   870
and cast a fair vote
and they respect the suppliants of Zeus
    this herd no one envies

HALFCHORUS Nor did they vote
supporting their own sex   and so
dishonor the fury of women

    For they considered Zeus
    Avenger's eye
    No battling that gaze, no house
    would have it light   880
    staining the thatch
    It perches heavy, hard

For they respect their kin
who supplicate Zeus
and their altars cleansed by reverence
    they shall delight heaven

HALFCHORUS O God!   though our mouths
lie in shadow   let our prayers
blaze far with friendblessing light

    Never may a plague   890
    of men drain this nation
    nor strife bloody Earth's breast
    with the bodies of her sons

Flower of youth   bud unstemmed
Ares Manmurderer
who heats Aphrodite's bed
must not mow down the finest blooms

HALFCHORUS And altarhearths
where greybeards cluster   let your fires
glow in bright welcome to wisdom   900

Nation!   be governed well
by godfearing men who
fear Zeus Guest and Stranger most
By greymaned law He casts our lots

Earthguardians!   rise evernew
throughout all time to come
Artemis! Hekate!   guard
women brought to bed with child

HALFCHORUS And no murderous
clanfeuds uprise   910
in this nation to divide it

      Danceless tuneless
      Tearbreeder Ares
      howls and clatters in the men who arm him

And Sickness   scttle your joyless
swarm far from the people's heads
And Apollo of Wolves   show mercy's bitc
to every tender child

HALFCHORUS And Zeus!   grant perfect
ripening to Earth's   920
fruit in every season

      And grazing cattle
      breed countless calves
      Earthpowers, skypowers nourish all who obey them

And altars   echo gladly poets'
godinvested hymns of thanks
And godbreathed prophecy   chant home to heaven
from tongues burnt clean by awe

HALFCHORUS Guard your mortal rights
      O citizens   Be unafraid   930

Here is the state's core and its strength:
your rule of foresight and concern for common good
And to all strangers give fair hearing
before grim Ares marches panoplied
Concede inviolate our godsent rights

HALFCHORUS This is home earth for gods
First, keep them blessed evermore
And praise them as your fathers did:
laurels highheld, oxen sacrificed, the rising smoke
And honor parents in supreme   940
obedience to the third commandment
written in godgiven law

DANAOS Sane prayers. I second them, my filial daughters.

Now let no witless panic rout you as you hear
a father's news of unexpected and rising danger.
From this high holy refuge the eye gazes far.
I see the ship.
                She is well marked.
I make no mistake: the cut of her canvas,
hide safety lines strung along the gunwales,   950
and the bow that has eyes for scanning the searoad
yet far too blindly answers directives
from the helm astern. She freights us no love.

How clear they are—manshapes, the crew, black
arms, legs stark against snowy uniforms.
And following, a fleet—escorts, troopships,
all glinting clear.
                The flagship has a wide lead;
she stands inshore, canvas already struck.
That steady clack of oars will soon bring her in.   960

But you must stay here making no noise.
Use self-control in facing this predicament.
Nor slight the gods.

And I shall come back when I've summoned
advocates who speak with swords,
in the event that someone—herald, deputation—
approaches, rough hands intent
on seizing you like stolen chattels.

NOT ONE SHALL DARE TOUCH YOU.
No need to dread them, no need to run. 970
Far better, should help's march be delayed,
never to forget the altar's present shield.

Courage.
Relentless time appoints the day, the very hour,
that godscorning flesh shall bow to vengeance.

A SUPPLIANT Father, I'm frightened   the ships   how swift
their wings   In time's midst, no time left

A SUPPLIANT Fear winds a sheet round my body
        Truth stops my breath
Far-racing flight   what was the earthly use? 980
My flesh feels thick and numb, I'm dying   Father!

DANAOS You are protected by the Argive vote.
They shall fight for you, I promise it, I know.

A SUPPLIANT They are a shoal of sharks   fleshmad   Egypt's sons
their battlethirst unslakable   This too you KNOW

A SUPPLIANT Hulls quest, shot spears, through the water
        Proweyes pierce the sea
The fin-sailed ships   too soon rage thrust them here
A legion, strong, stormblack   rides in their bellies

DANAOS And it shall meet a legion, whose sword-arms 990
have been honed to muscle by hard work.

A SUPPLIANT To be alone!   Don't leave me, Father   please
A woman alone, a nothing   empty of war

A SUPPLIANT But THEY are
       blood-impelled and born to treachery and
       crammed with unclean hungers   carrion crows   to whom
       altars mean nothing

DANAOS (*pointing to the trident*) But how useful to us, children,
       if they make the gods hate them.

A SUPPLIANT No godspear   no sign glorious to the gods   1000
       will cut their grasp on us   FATHERRRR

A SUPPLIANT For THEY are
       blood-obsessed   wound fast in shameless heat
       slavering and fleshcrazed   brazen dogs   that know
       nothing of gods

DANAOS It's said that wolves are stronger than dogs,
       that papyrus cannot seed the grainfields.

                                   He descends from the sanctuary.

A SUPPLIANT Casual lusts, easy angers own them   They are
       animals   empty of the laws that heaven gives men

A SUPPLIANT I must guard myself quickly!   1010

          The SUPPLIANTS *cluster around* DANAOS, *who indicates*
              that they must again take sanctuary. They hesitate,
                          reluctant to let him go.

DANAOS Not quick at all, the arrayal of a seaborne taskforce
       nor its mooring. Sternropes must be hauled ashore
       before they're made fast, and when the anchors bite in,
       not even then are the ships' herdsmen satisfied,
       especially if they've made a portshy coast
       after the sun begins its stride toward night. And Night
       likes mothering birthpains in the watchful helmsman.
       I see no army successfully debouched

until the ships themselves feel snug at their moorings.   1020
And you, be cautious though fear beats at you.
Do not neglect your gods.
                              [I will return]
as soon as help is mustered. A call to arms—
no, the people won't reproach its clarion,
an old man lent youth by his quick-tongued wits.

    He exits right. The SUPPLIANTS *linger on the level ground.*

HALFCHORUS io io ioioioioio
    O Earth
      O healing hills
        Allholy law whence comes my strength   1030
    what shall I suffer?
      Where shall I flee in this country
    of pastures?   Is there a dark burrow?

    Let my blackness be smoke
    sister to God's clouds
      All unseen
      let me whirl up
      secrct as wingless dust
          Let me be lost

HALFCHORUS io io ioioioioio   1040
    No flight
      no time to hide
        Inhuman cruelty leaves no escape
    My heart beats darker
      dashes like a small trapped creature
    A father's eye snares me, fear haunts me

    Let my bondage to doom
    end in a slipnoose
      Before a man
      I wish unborn   1050

can touch my flesh, O come
$\qquad$ husband me, Death

HALFCHORUS How shall I reach a throne in mid-air
$\qquad$ where the clouds' white night turns to snow?
Or a sheer slick
$\qquad$ goatfoiling
$\qquad$ unpointed out
$\qquad$ lone-spirited
$\qquad$ vulture-reeling peak
to jut in witness $\hfill$ 1060
$\qquad$ above my valleyed corpse?

$\qquad$ Must I be forced against heart's dream
$\qquad$ into a murderous bed?

HALFCHORUS No! first dogs shall eat and birds make feast
$\qquad$ A godless grave, I do not care
To die, to ease
$\qquad$ free from wail-
$\qquad$ exciting pain
$\qquad$ Cease, doomed breath
$\qquad$ Come come, Death, before $\hfill$ 1070
that other dying
$\qquad$ in the bridal room

$\qquad$ What saving channel must I cut
$\qquad$ to escape a marriage bed?

HALFCHORUS Toll, doomcry, on the sky's bluest shores
$\qquad$ Tell tell the gods
$\qquad$ I wail for my dying
Make it true
$\qquad$ Release me
$\qquad$ Heal me of storms $\hfill$ 1080
Look peace on me, Father
$\qquad$ Whose lawgiving eye
looks no light on brute force

               Send blessings to those
               who entreat You
               Earthcradler Allguiding Zeus

                    Offstage, men's voices grunt and shout.

HALFCHORUS Egypt's get, how ugly their self-glory
                    how hardpressing
                         their misbegot maleness
               I have fled   1090
                    They track me
                         Found earth
               They bay and they clamor
                                        with lawbreaking lust
               to take me by brute force

               Zeus! You hold the scales
               Who other than You
               can steady the deathbound?

                    The SUPPLIANTS *run to the foot of the sanctuary
                         and begin to climb.*

A SUPPLIANT No   No   No   NO NO-O-O-O-O

A SUPPLIANT Rapists   seafoulers   shorecrawlers   1100

A SUPPLIANT Before you take me   die die die

SPOKESMAN (*offstage*) Down.   Come down, you.   Now.

A SUPPLIANT Cry cry   fill air with anguish
               I see looming shadows   acts of pain
               force impaling me

SUPPLIANTS   No   No   NONONONONO

A SUPPLIANT Climb   fly   HERE is our only strength

A SUPPLIANT Beasthearted lechery burdening the sea the shore

The Egyptian SPOKESMAN *and an armed guard enter left.*

SUPPLIANTS Lord on earth   stand before us

SPOKESMAN Sssssssssssssssssssss———   1110

So.   You.   Move move.   To the ship's
boat.   On your feet.   HUP

You won't, won't you?

Hair torn, torn out, skin stung.
Bloodrivers, you beg for murder.
Chopnecks, toppleheads,
move.   Move!
                    Then be damned, damn you,
                    there on your dunghill.

A SUPPLIANT I wish   1120
                weltering waves had
                    flooded the saltroad
            and you   with your slavemaster's self-love
            and you   in your brassbolted hulls
                    I wish you had foundered

[SUPPLIANTS Rather bleed   sweeten this hill with my death
            than go down to the ship]

[EGYPTIANS Bloody hill   reek of death
            Go down to the ship]

SPOKESMAN I order: stop this madmouth   1130
            crazy woman cursing.
            You and you, all of you,
            get up, march down to the landing craft.

You—honorless, homeless,
not worth my love or fear.

A SUPPLIANT I wish
      you never again see
         the springflooding water
Only there   can you trade your cattle for brides
Only there   can your lifebearing blood   1140
         arrive at full flower

[SUPPLIANTS My earth is here   my old and noble line
      my home my throne]

[EGYPTIANS My earth   my line
      your home is mine]

SPOKESMAN You, yes, you'll board the ship
and fast, willing, unwilling,
forced alive, forced till life runs out.
[Shegoats are for covering and giving birth,
and then for butchering.]   1150

A SUPPLIANT ah-aiaiai
      that you
         were hard-driven   helplessly lost
          in the holy blue groves of Ocean
         wind-battered   cast aground
         your wanderings tombed
          in a wilderness of spumy sand

SPOKESMAN Yowl and caterwaul and clamor at the gods.
There's no outleaping Egypt's craft.
Yelp and bleat.   Keep on.   1160
Add bite to your dreary noise.

                                    He starts climbing.

A SUPPLIANT oh-ohohohoh
      how you

lash upward   brooling bloodlust
  a crocodile bloated with sureness
The Nile moves   vast in you
May it wind away
  from that morass where your self-blindness thrives

The SPOKESMAN *reaches the sanctuary.*

SPOKESMAN Go down, I order it.   Board the boat.
Its eyes turn home.   1170
Fast as you can.   No more loitering.
Dragging has no love for ladycurls.

A SUPPLIANT Oh-oi   Father!   Godstones' rescue
      cheats me   Saltward he presses
        spiderish   one step, two
            Dream!   Black   dream!

SUPPLIANTS OTOTOTOI   MA GA   MAAA   GAAAA

A SUPPLIANT Mama   Earth   Mother me
                                        His snarl
      I'm scared   Keep him away   1180
      O Pa   Earth-child   O God!

SPOKESMAN I fear none of your demonhost.
They didn't give me suck,
won't nurse me to my old age.

A SUPPLIANT Lustmad   deathmad   he winds closer
        hissing   two-leggèd mansnake
          pit viper   striking out
              Fangs   hold   tight

He grasps her arm.

SUPPLIANTS OTOTOTOI   MA GA MA GA MA GAAAA

A SUPPLIANT MA GA   EARTH   MOTHER ME   1190

His clutch

I'm scared   Tear him away
O PA   GAS PAI   ZEU!

SPOKESMAN If none of you agrees to board ship,
then ripping shows no pity for your skirts.

He does as he says.

A SUPPLIANT Generals   princes of my people
I am breaking

SPOKESMAN Be dragged by your pullaway hair.
You are not quick enough to catch my words.

A SUPPLIANT Hope dies   High lord, I live on in pain   1200
beyond speaking

SPOKESMAN Many lords, sons of Egypt,
soon you'll see them every one.
Here's comfort:
you won't squeal then that you lack rule.

PELASGOS *enters right with a company of soldiers.*
The SPOKESMAN *descends from the sanctuary.*

PELASGOS Who are you? What
are you doing? What presumption
leads you to defile a country rich in men?
Do you think you come to a nation of women?
Savage,   1210
you insult Greeks far too carelessly.
Your fancies mistake their target;
not one flies straight.

SPOKESMAN Have I done anything unlawful?

PELASGOS Strangers should behave decently. You don't.

SPOKESMAN How not? I find lost property and take it.

PELASGOS Who protects your interests here?

SPOKESMAN Hermes the Searcher, a master protector.

PELASGOS Your tone is irreverent.

SPOKESMAN I left my reverence beside the Nile.   1220

PELASGOS You mean, these gods are nothing?

SPOKESMAN I'll take my women if no one spirits them away.

PELASGOS You'll howl for mercy if you touch them.

SPOKESMAN Strangers deserve a better welcome.

PELASGOS Not strangers who rob the gods.

SPOKESMAN Those words will anger Egypt's sons.

PELASGOS Don't threaten me.

SPOKESMAN But the more I know, the more clear my report;
my duty is to bear exact intelligence.
What shall I tell them? Who steals for himself   1230
this company of women, our own blood cousins?

Ares does not judge a case
by hearing windy words. He takes no silver
to blunt men's swords. Before the end comes:
many thudding bodies, many kicked-off lives.

PELASGOS What need to give you my name?
In time you shall learn it,
you and your shipmates, and learn it well.

Yet, with their heartfelt, reasoning consent,
you still may take the women if—   1240
   if godfear comes alive in your inducements.

But my assembled people, voting as one,
have shown their will:
   This mission of women shall never
   be surrendered into forceful hands.
And a nail is so exactly driven
through that promise, it shall hold everfast.

None of this is published
   on deepcarved stone or bronze
nor sealed in the pages of official documents.   1250
Clear facts:
   you hear the truth voiced freely by a candid man.

Get yourself gone. You foul my sight.

SPOKESMAN I warn: you bind yourself to new bonecracking war.
Victory, power, glory! Let them come to real men.

PELASGOS Men, yes. My earth supports fullblooded men.
Here you'll find no breed that swills malt-wine.

The SPOKESMAN *and his company exeunt left.*

(*to the* SUPPLIANTS)
You are all in the care of friends.
Retrieve your brave hopes. Come
   to the city's safekeeping.   1260
Thick stones circle it, the towers
   grow from deepest roots.
Come with me now.

The SUPPLIANTS *do not respond.*

Do you wonder where you'll live?
Many houses offer ample public lodging,

and I myself am not housed in pinched quarters.
We are ready to welcome you as honored guests
in any of our lively households. But,
    if you prefer,
you may choose to live alone, sequestered quietly.   1270
Whichever best pleases you, enheartens you most,
pick that flower.
    We shield and defend you,
I and all my countrymen, whose vote has taken
full effect. Come.
                        Why wait? For higher authority?

A SUPPLIANT   May goodness blossom to reward your goodness,
              most godly of men.
              But send, please send us
              our father, sureminded Danaos,   1280
              prophet and heart's guide.
              His plans grow from judgment far richer than ours.
              He knows where we should live
              and knows the city welcomes us
              and knows that people anywhere will cry
              blame on the foreign-tongued.

                  Let everyone be pleased
                  and no one angrily defame
                  our innocence.

                        PELASGOS *and his soldiers exeunt right.*

Sisters, my friends and my sisters, be calm.   1290
Our father allots each one her dowry:
to serve a virgin future.

                        DANAOS *enters right with an escort of spearmen*
                                and a chorus of ARGIVE WOMEN.

DANAOS   Children,
         we must thank the people of Argos with prayers
         and sacrificed animals and red wine outpoured

as if we thanked the highest gods.
These mortal men are saviors, weighed
and found not wanting.

My account of our trials moved them to support their kin
and fired their bitterness against your cousins.   1300
For me they marshalled this flourish of skilled spears
that I might have the honor due my rank
and not be ambushed by spearkilling fate, and die,
for then my living ghost would place a burden on the land.

They have rescued you.
From the helm of virtue thank them,
praise them with chastity,
increase their honor by preserving yours

Now write these words,
add them to the treasury   1310
of paternal maxims written earlier on your minds:
An unknown congregation is tested by time.
People everywhere are quick to wag
cruel tongues against an alien;
with ease they speak befouling slander.
You have my warning:
do not shame me.

There glows in you a season that makes men turn and hunger.
The succulence of summerfruit is never guarded well enough.
Animals paw it, batten on it; so do men. Why not?   1320
Some monsters soar and strike, others roam earth on two feet.
[When the fruit blushes ripe, Aphrodite bells a summons
and sets out feasts behind downtrampled gates.]
And when voluptuousness shapes unmated beauty,
every passing eye shoots arrows of enticement
as every passing man falls victim to base appetites.

Be circumspect.
We have already sailed

high seas and seas of trouble
to leave behind *that* suffering.   1330
Our disgrace would feed joy in my enemies.
New lives are near, and a twofold gift of houses,
in virgin cloisters or among the people.
The way of life we choose shall cost us
nothing but sustained decorum.
Easy terms!

But one last warning:
guard a father's commandments;
love your chastity more than your lives.

SUPPLIANTS I pray the high gods look fortune upon me.   1340
And summer's fruit?
                        Be trustful, Father.
Unless godplans have sent new storms onspinning,
my heart shall not be turned from its first-followed path.

They take their branches from the altar and descend from
the sanctuary.

Go forth in brightness exalting
    home's highest lords
the blest gods
        who guard the lifestream of the nation
        who hallow the landloving rivers
    till their agelong white rush enters the sea   1350

Believe!   all you who attend us
    receive
our choired promise
        Fame shall embrace this city and people
        No more shall we sing hymns to quell Nile
    spilling its siltflood into the sea

Sing praise to rivers that rise here
    and thrust through homefields
the sun-oiled streams
        that here shed their pleasurous waters   1360

to sweeten the dust of the mother Earth
and fulfill her with life upon life

But see us!   unbroken Artemis
    be fierce
for our voyage
        Help us withstand the womb's urge to fullness
        that opens virgins to Aphrodite's act
    Out of that prize wells the river of death

ARGIVE WOMEN But Aphrodite is not scanted here
        nor do her rites lack eager celebrants.   1370
    She wields such lightning that she,
        with heaven's queen, stands next to Zeus.
    And she is thanked, guile-dazzling
        goddess, for her solemn games.
    And in her motherlight soft daughters walk,
        Passion and one who brooks no denial,
        spellchanting Persuasion.
    To Union then is given the share of love
        that touches and whispers
    and follows the well-traveled paths.   1380

    But you are fugitives. And fear for you
        sends chills of warning through the summerheat.
    Somewhere a storm gathers dark breath:
        cruelty and suffering and bloodblack war.
    What good the fair winds of your passage
        that also sped heelnipping hounds?
    Fate spins each beginning to its only end.
        The Godmind's mystery is impassable;
        no man may overreach it.
    And now, as it has ever been and shall be,   1390
        marriage is destiny,
    and a woman's consummate crown.

A SUPPLIANT Zeus!   O cover me conceal me
        Marry Egypt's brood?
                        I cannot

A WOMAN But marrying would best serve peace.

A SUPPLIANT You chant spells to the spelldeaf.

A WOMAN YOU know nothing of the future.

A SUPPLIANT How can I futuregaze Zeus' mind?
             His eye holds the abyss   1400
                              It blinds me

A WOMAN Be temperate when you cry to Him!

A SUPPLIANT What will that teaching profit me?

A WOMAN To claim no special grace from heaven.

SUPPLIANTS Zeus!   Lord on high!   deprive me
           of marriage   man-built prison
           that stabs and kills
                         It was Your breath
           that transfigured Io   It was
           Your hand   1410
                         healing, triumphant
                                        that held her
           down as You planted Your sweet force

           Glory and power   stream them
           on women   Better the half-light
           than utter dark
                         That I accept
           for heaven's law follows   the lawful
           My hands
                         see! no wrong stains them   1420
                                        O save me
           God, end and beginning of help

                         The SUPPLIANTS *hold their branches high.*
                              ALL *exeunt slowly, ceremoniously right.*

70

TRANSLATOR'S NOTES
NOTES ON THE TEXT
GLOSSARY

TRANSLATOR'S NOTES

A WARNING

In honor of Aeschylus the translation stays as close to fifth-century concepts as it can without becoming just one more piece of word-for-word prose broken into lines that have the appearance but not the substance of poetry. Here, however, are some of the unGreek, unstoppable ideas that rose in my mind during the three years that I lived deeply with *Suppliants*. All are personal views. None will enlighten the student who tries to understand the workings of Greek tragedy. Some might help a director re-create the play, though I cannot imagine, can only hope, that it will someday be given the physical translation of a performance.

Little is certain about the original staging and actors' masks. Ancient rumor reports that Aeschylus was a master of spectacle. The early classical stage on which *Suppliants* was probably performed is described briefly in section II of the Introduction. Through Danaos (226) Aeschylus asked his audience to imagine that the raised stage was a rocky height. We do know that real statues of the gods and a real altar stood on that stage. And here knowledge ends, fancy begins.

THE ULTIMATE QUESTION

Suppliants is a play of many questions. The hardest to answer is, Can it be translated? Transformed and transfigured, made human again, without losing its mystery and poetry? How can anyone now hope to find the right, charged words when Aeschylus has already found them? If only everyone could read Greek! How, in a secular age, can anyone be brought to believe in the holiness that indwells words, rivers, sea, earth, sky, stones, pastures, cows? If only everyone were Greek!

COWS

The fact that I grew up with cows has made more trouble for me in coming to grips with *Suppliants* than any single problem in the play itself. All my life I've known cows—Guernseys, Jerseys, Holsteins, Herefords, Angus, Charolais. The word cow has always been denotative. It triggers memories of real moos and bawls, clanking stanchions, hoofs stomping straw-covered concrete, the swish of flywhisk tails, mucus-damp noses, calf-tongues rasping my fingers, shaggy patable winter coats. Dull silver tags clipped on golden ears. The fusty sweet warm snuffling dark of a cowbarn at night. Tests for Bang's disease and TB. I know that sturdy bovine bodies are slung from bony ridgepoles totally unsuited to bareback riding. I know that in an Ohio springtime raw milk has a special April flavor of onion grass. Barn cats like it; I don't. And I know that milk cows can be intractable about letting down milk to inexperienced fingers. Milking takes the dexterity of a pianist and the knotty strength of an Indian wrestler; my twelfth summer was a summer of aching forearms. Granted, some cows, especially the beef breeds, can be mighty mean, but I've always known Cow in general as a plodding, gentle ungulate whose miracle is that quadripartite stomach. Cow has never, ever, seemed frightening and tragic.

I read *Suppliants* clean to mid-play with old friends Boss and Caramel chewing their cuds and supplying prosaic mental pictures for Io. Why could she not have been transformed into a beautiful animal, a deer or a tawny lioness? It was no help to remember that in ancient Greece sheep and goats were the common domestic animals and only rich men, aristocrats and Homeric kings, maintained herds of cattle.

And then, in the Suppliants' account of her torment and deliverance, Io came alive. Half-cow, half-woman, she was not the lumbering barnyard animal I know but a magical creature who epitomized a true and crippling human condition, who was healed of her sickness. What was that condition? Back to play's beginning and a re-reading of myth's implications. Faith was placed in Aeschylus the poet rather than in the latter-day dicta of people who deal in prose. Lexicographers, especially, tell unintended lies; the alphabetically entombed verb is not the verb given life by rhythm and context. I relied instead on intuition and gave imagination its head. A risky act.

Twice I've seen calves die of exuberance. Both, released from the barn into the first springtime of their lives, leaped and ran, crazy with sun and new grass, and careered into the pasture gate and broke their necks.

THE GODS

I see, I feel:

A time of spirit that transcends finite body-time.

A place that is called Argos but can be any place of hot light and heart's darkness.

A beach and a central mound of earth where immense god-images are gathered: a sunburst, a trident, a winged phallos, an eagle with wings upstretched as if it had just fallen from heaven upon its prey. The names of the gods in this world are Sun and Ocean and Fool, and the greatest of them all is simply God. In front of their images is the low stone rectangle of their flame-crowned altar. Behind them, not concealed by them, is a fifth image that serves a dramatic purpose in imagination, though it is not mentioned in *Suppliants'* catalogue (260-68): a round earth-shape with a figure curled motionless in its central hollow. All the images are capable of movement, all are alive.

THE SONS OF EGYPT

Over and again the Suppliants describe the Egyptians in animal terms. Io's grandsons are dogs, carrion crows, spiders, pit vipers, a wingèd horde, a black dream out of Egypt. Egypt, yes. Apis, Anubis, Set, and Thoth. The sons' torsos and limbs are human, but their heads are animal—bull, jackal, snake, lion, vulture, baboon, crocodile. They appear on imagination's stage like divine beasts or brutalized gods, apparitions from an adolescent's erotic daydreams.

A POSTLUDE

Suppliants' unbroken tensions oppress its readers. Is it possible to restore the play a little to its ancient serial context? Can I use here the plastic method I've used to recombine and translate archaic Latin lines that have lost their poems? The Latin lines arranged themselves by imagery and themes into groups that could be translated as complete poems. To break and end the storm, to release myself, I have taken the fragments mentioned in section III of the Introduction and imagined a postlude. Here, for the curious, are the fragment numbers given by H. Weir Smyth, *Aeschylus*, volume II, Loeb Classical Library, Harvard University Press, 1926: 197, 223, 206, 162, 163, 24 (wedding customs), 223, 208, and 25 (Aphrodite's benediction). Zagreus, the single word left from the second play, was suggested by Garvie, p. 163. It is an epithet of Dionysos, god of wine and manic ecstasy. Its use in the play is unknown, but it piques my fancy because it was associated with a bull-form of Dionysos and with flesh-eating rites.

The Suppliants, Danaos, and their attendants *exeunt* right. The stage is deserted for seconds, minutes. The light begins to darken toward a feeling of late afternoon, first streaks of sunset on the sky. The sons of Egypt in full battledress enter left, their animal heads cruel against the grey and rose. The sounds are those of military precision, armor clanking rhythmically, feet marching in measured cadence. And the Egyptians *exeunt* right. The stage is again empty of everyone but the gods. The sunset reddens. Offstage sounds of battle rise, peak, and give way to the lamentations of women.

SUPPLIANTS Io io ioioioioiooooooo
          You   YOU sowed my life, YOU would lay it waste.

DANAOS It pleases God to spend His might for the troubleworn.
          The sons of Egypt, true, weave clever snares.
          But there are subterfuges heaven sanctions.
          God shall not stand aside.
          There is a season, too, for lies.
          And God shall honor them.

          When sun's first clear light stanches rosy dawn,
          I will wake you, as custom bids,
          and the bridegrooms whose sleep you have
          enchanted with the grace deserved.
          And may this night bear heavy fruit.
          Courage.   God lends His might to the troubleworn.

Silence. The sky turns to a bloody night. A woman cries out inarticulately, and the gods surrounding the altar come alive, glittering, bending, whirling. The altar-fire swells and leaps. This is murder's hour.

SUPPLIANTS ZAGREUS

>GOD

>>HUNTER

>>>HELP US HELP US

>>>>HELP US

At their height the invocations suddenly cease. The altar-fire dwindles, the gods become still. The Suppliants, cloaked and veiled, enter right with Danaos.

DANAOS Children,
circle the altar and its beckoning flame,
and, yourselves encircled
by the gods' escapeless, everlasting battleranks,
for your unbedded innocence
give thankful praise.

The Suppliants, followed by their father, climb to the sanctuary and stand before the gods. Danaos approaches his daughters, and in turn they tear off their veils, their faces are only half-human, horns sprout from their heads. Proudly they whip forth obedient bloody hands. He nods, his pleasure wordless and lunatic, until he sees that the last pair of hands is clean, the face whole. The one surviving bridegroom enters right, his animal mask in his hands, and his face is as beautiful as that of Osiris risen. And out of the one god-image that has not moved, the earth-shape, the goddess Love uncurls herself, stretches, and stands.

LOVE Desire   yes   Sky's holy quickfire longs
to pierce the curvèd world
Desire desire   grips Earth and reels her
toward the coupling
And Sky's rain   showered in their blissful bed
impregnates Earth
And she gives birth   the herds' grass and the grain
for man's joy and continuing
By that torrential wedding   life learns its seasons
the sprout, the flower, the completed fruit
And I am the divine accomplice
Love

                                                        J.L.

NOTES ON THE TEXT

1 *ZEUS MEN APHIKTOR*   The Suppliants' initial cry to Zeus is transliterated
from the Greek. It means, roughly, *Zeus of Suppliants* or *Zeus Sup-
pliant-Protector.*

1-2 *Shining Father/Protector of suppliants; Our father on earth*   The first phrase
is an expanded gloss on the transliterated Greek; the word for father
does not appear in the text. The literal reading of the second phrase
(l. 14) is *Danaos father.* The Greek, however, contains a pair of par-
ticles—*men/de,* on the one hand/on the other—that contrasts the
names of Zeus and Danaos. Because fatherhood is an important issue
in the play, it seems fair to emphasize the contrast in translation.

3 *voyage of women*   I have used *voyage* as a collective noun to translate the Greek
word *stolos,* company or band or troop. The Suppliants have, after
all, just completed a sea journey.

6 *boundaries graze desert*   The Greek reads *Syria,* not *desert.* But in my pursuit
of the evocative word I have decided to use a word suggesting the
harshness the Suppliants fled rather than to retain a concrete geographical reference that does not again appear in the play.

11-13 *escaping self-built prisons for our own flesh . . . the unholy thought*   The
lines, not at all clear in Greek, have been the subject of much scholarly conjecture. Do the Suppliants loathe only the idea of marrying
the Egyptians? Or do they hate all men, all thoughts of marriage? I
suspect that an intrinsic poetic ambiguity is in part responsible for
these questions. The Suppliants do reject marriage to the Egyptians,
and they express this rejection in terms that conjure the Io-history.
There is, I think, a comparison of their own plight with that of Io:
marriage would imprison them much as Io was held under Argos'

neversleeping guard. The crucial, implicit difference is that Io's captivity was divinely devised, divinely ended, while marriage would be a captivity the Suppliants would take upon themselves without hope of heavenly intervention. Aigyptos is called Egypt throughout the translation.

14 *Our father on earth*   No one knows today at what point Danaos originally made his entrance. It has been placed at play's beginning or immediately prior to his first speech. I see him enter, however, when his name is first mentioned.

28-9 *With these mightiest swords . . . branches flowering white unspun wool*   The latent ferocity of the Suppliants glints briefly here in the comparison of their suppliant emblems to weapons that can kill. And in tragedy death dealt by a sharp blade was a typically feminine form of murder. The Greek is more pointed; it uses a word that means *dagger*, not *sword*.

30 *O home*   The Greek says *O polis. Polis* is a loaded word that is all too often flatly translated as *city*. But the ancient *polis* was more, much more, than a collection of stones and timbers. The word rather describes a social organization, a way of life, and by extension can be read as referring to the *place* in which social life was lived. According to context, I have translated *polis* in many ways: home, people, nation, state, and, yes, as city when the material aspect of *polis* seems uppermost.

33 *Saviour Zeus*   Zeus, all-knowing and all-experiencing, has many aspects and many epithets. In *Suppliants* he also appears as Zeus Aphiktor (1), Father Allvisioning (152), First Father (254), Zeus Suppliant (425, 480, 841), Zeus Jury-Appointer (444), Zeus Alldestroyer (529), Wealthguarding Zeus (576), Zeus Guest and Stranger (856 and 903), Zeus Avenger (878), and Earthcradler (1086).

40 *self-vaunting*   Here Aeschylus writes *hybris*.

47 *decency forbid*   The Greek calls upon Themis, the moral basis of law and justice.

50-201 *O be joyful now sing . . . blows a night of storm*   The Suppliants' first and longest ode begins in joy but soon turns eerily, prophetically, into lamentation. Laments are far from unusual in Greek tragedy. It is suggestive to remember that tragedies were performed at festivals that took place in the spring and that spring is a time of both grief and joy. Christianity's Holy Week provides a familiar analogue in its mourning for Christ crucified and its celebration of His resurrection. The Suppliants, however, move from happiness to sorrow.

For those who are interested in such matters, it may be helpful to explain a little about choral odes and the ways in which I try to re-create the odes of *Suppliants*. In classical Greek practice such odes were tightly patterned in paired stanzas—a strophe that is followed by an antistrophe repeating the metrical structure. The terms strophe and antistrophe are now both used with the sense of "stanza," but they mean "turn" and "counterturn" and presumably referred to the dance movements of the Chorus. In choral lyrics strophe and anti-strophe may be accompanied by an epode, an "after-ode." The three epodes of *Suppliants* are found near the end of the first long lamentation, and they can easily be distinguished because they act as a reiterated refrain. In all the odes sung by the Suppliants, words and ideas that occur in the strophe often recur significantly in the anti-strophe; sometimes they occupy similar, if not identical, positions in the lines. Lines 766 and 778-79 provide an example: Zeus "Who lives without end" and his son Epaphos "who lived a life crowned with years and gold." Such correspondences are readily translated. The Greek meters, however, cannot be reproduced in English because the sound-properties of the languages are intrinsically different. But to convey some idea of the discipline that informs the Greek, I have translated each strophe and its antistrophe into twin stanzas linked by close syllabic and rhythmic similarities.

58 *Epaphos, Caress-born*   The proper name Epaphos signifies *touch* or *caress*.

71-9 *to her who was wife . . . own hand's anger unmothered*   The Suppliants here combine two ancient nightingale stories. In the text they speak of the wife of Tereus, Aēdōn, whose name is the Greek word for nightingale. In the *Odyssey* (xix.518ff.) Homer briefly mentions a nightingale, *aēdōn*, once wife of Zethus, who killed her son Itylos and ever after on spring nights sang in lamentation. Tereus, king of Thrace, figures in a bloodier myth told by Apollodorus (iii.14.8) and Achilles Tatius (v.3, 5). Pandion, king of Athens, had two daughters, Procne and Philomela, and to reward Tereus for helping him in battle, he gave Procne in marriage to the Thracian. She bore him one son, Itys. But she was lonely in barbaric Thrace and sent Tereus to Athens to bring her sister for a visit. On the journey north Tereus raped Philomela and cut out her tongue to keep her from telling Procne of the assault. Philomela, however, wove a tapestry that pictured the event. And Procne sought revenge. She killed Itys, boiled him, and served him as dinner to her faithless husband. The sisters fled, but Tereus, soon realizing what he had eaten, seized an axe and hunted them down. When they saw his murderous rage, they prayed that the gods turn them into birds. Prayer was answered. Philomela became a songless swallow, and Procne a nightingale whose trill, *ity ity*, repeats the name of her dead son. And Tereus, changed to a hawk, hunts them still.

80 *And singing Io's song*   The literal reading is *lamentation in Ionian measures* or *in the Ionian mode*, a direct reference to musical practice. But the adjective *Ionian* certainly evokes Io. And the Greek word *nomos* that I have translated as *song* is close in sound to a word signifying *pasture*. Aristophanes makes a pun on the correspondence in *The Birds*, l. 1287.

88 *who will here lament and bury us?*   This entire line interprets a single Greek word, *kēdemōn*. Translators of this play have let it off too lightly as *kinsman* or *protector*, which is its classical sense. But I look back to Homer, who uses the word only for someone who is charged with the care and ritual burial of the dead. In the context of *Suppliants* it seems most appropriate to see it as signifying "a person with enough family feeling to see that mourning and burial are properly performed." (Thank you, Margaret Alexiou, for your concurring letter.)

90 *heaven's laws*   Here and elsewhere the words translate references to the concept of *dikē*.

98-107 *And Zeus! grant that my hopes all come true . . . that men cannot read*   Editors vary in their arrangements of these lines. I have followed Johansen's order.

126 *alalala*   Greek tragedy has a large store of grieving cries, and the Suppliants wail many of them. Some I have simply transliterated: *aiai, otototoi*. Others have been adapted to the needs of the English: *ulululu* for the Greek *iō iō*; *away away away* for the Greek *eé*. Exactly such in-

articulate expressions of grief may be heard today on the tongues of Greek village women.

130 *Hillpastures*   The Greek words are *Apian bounin;* the literal reading is *Apian land-of-hills,* an apparently straightforward description. But the words reverberate. The adjective *Apian,* as applied to Argos' hills, summons the healer Apis who came to Argos and cured the polluted earth (331 and 342). And *bounin,* a rare word, calls to mind the Greek word for cow, *bous.*

131 *My cry holds Egypt's savagery*   I have given this line a double meaning that may not exist in the Greek. *Egypt's savagery* can refer both to the Suppliants' foreign-flavored Greek and to the savage murderousness that sleeps within them.

132 *Mother-earth*   Again there are two references, one to the primal Gaia, the goddess Earth, and the other to the home earth of the Suppliants' maternal ancestor Io.

134-5 *the fine-spun veil/that shrouds my sight*   The passage in Greek refers to nothing other than the physical action the Suppliants perform to accompany their words. In a traditional gesture of mourning they rip their veils of "fine Sidonian linen," as the Greek has it. I have gone beyond these bounds to suggest the Suppliants' blindness to their plight.

136-8 *But rites for the dead . . . bearing a bloodcurse*   The storm-shadow darkens. The Suppliants know their premature sorrow is an act of ill omen, but uncontrollably they persist in lamentation. The same superstition figures in the *Iliad* (vi.500) and at least five other tragedies, Aeschylus' *Persians,* Sophocles' *Elektra* and *Antigone,* Euripides' *Alcestis* and *Hecuba.* Here the picture is especially chilling, for the Suppliants mourn themselves.

160 *stainless daughter of Zeus*   Artemis is the goddess invoked. The text does not name her, nor is it now clear about what, exactly, she is doing. The Greek seems to see her as holding a shrine wall securely or keeping her face safely. I have chosen the former image for its sexual suggestiveness in relation to the Suppliants' predicament.

180 *gods on the skysummits*   Olympos is the summit mentioned in the text.

208-9 *for I see/dust*   Danaos describes what he actually sees and at the same time seems to prophesy the advent of the Egyptian army that will, after this play ends, vanquish Argos.

254 *Zeus! First Father*   The Greek says *Zeus Progenitor.* I wish to suggest both his divine fatherhood and his actual fathering of the Suppliants' line.

258-61 *O God, this weariness . . . Praise takes wing, flies toward the sun*   Though the meaning of this passage seems clear in the Greek, the arrangement of the lines is uncertain, and one line spoken by the Suppliants is known to be missing. I have followed the Loeb order. The missing line is ignored, for conjecture would here add nothing to the general tone of troubled invocation.

262 *And Apollo, god who spent a year on earth*   Myth says that Apollo's son, the physician Asklepios, once used his healing powers to bring a man back from the dead. This misapplication of godgiven skill enraged Zeus, who hurled his lethal thunderbolt through doctor and patient. In retaliation for his son's death Apollo killed the thunderbolt-makers, the Cyclopes. For this act Zeus condemned Apollo to everlasting punishment in Hades, but Leto, Apollo's mother, interceded and the sentence was commuted to a year of shepherding the earthly flocks of King Admetos.

273 *pitying of doves*   The Greek says a *swarm of doves,* using the same word that denotes the Egyptian *manswarm* (*swarm of males* in literal translation) and brings to mind Io's tormenting fly. But I could not resist here employing an old and genuine collective term—as genuine as covey of quail and murder of crows—that both describes the Suppliants as a group and says something about their state of mind.

286 *final vengeance*   The Greek refers to *dikē,* which both benefits and punishes.

291 PELASGOS   By a curious inversion that may have held no significance whatever for the poet or the original Greek audience, Aeschylus chose to name the Greek king "Pelasgos." Some versions of the myth give the king's name as Gelanor. Pelasgos, in *Suppliants* the archetypal Greek, was, in Greek legend, the eponymous ruler of a pre-Greek people, the Pelasgi, who inhabited the mainland during that time now called the Neolithic and whose non-Greek language and ways persisted in isolated pockets well into classical times. Aeschylus presents Danaos, on the other hand, as a black foreigner. Danaos was, to be sure, of

Greek descent, but his line was four generations removed from Argos. Yet, it is the alien Danaos whose name is given, in Homer and elsewhere, to the Danaans. And Danaans is simply a generic term for Greeks.

294-5 *and womanly, yet gaudy as no women/I have ever known or dreamed* Pelasgos says literally, "Not Argolid your women's dress, nor from any place in Hellas." He implies that the Suppliants' appearance is beyond his experience and imagining, and so have I translated.

313 *Ancient Ground* Palaikhthon is the ancestral name given by Pelasgos. Uncapitalized it is a compound word that means nothing other than ancient-ground, ancient-land. Pelasgos is not, however, saying merely that he was born on Argive soil. Rather, he claims descent from a divine son of the goddess Earth.

315-17 *and I/for these good reasons stand first/among the land's many sons* The Greek yields, "And for me, their king, the tribe of the Pelasgi . . . is appropriately named." Pelasgos is telling the Suppliants indirectly that he is not an absolute king but a leader, *primus inter pares.* The Suppliants, unfamiliar with Argive government, do not catch his meaning.

319-27 *Over plains, over valleys . . . until sea restrains me/with its bluesalt marches* Aeschylus' geography is more specific than mine. According to Johansen's edition, the Greek says, "And over all the region through which pure Strymon flows—there toward the setting sun, I rule. And I am bounded by the Paionians' land that lies beyond Pindos, near the Perrhaibians and the mountains of Dodona. And the boundary of the moist sea cuts me short." Pelasgos claims territory far north of the Argolid peninsula. Strymon is a river in Thrace. Pindos is a mountain range in northwestern Greece. Dodona, renowned seat of a pre-Greek oracle, lies in Epirus. Because the names of tribes and places are non-evocative in English and would only, at best, send a few diligent readers to a map, I have tried less concretely to suggest the immensity of Pelasgos' claims.

329-42 *And the region around us . . . his reproachless name a fee of prayer* Argos and Egypt are in many ways linked in *Suppliants,* and these lines show a most subtle connection. The Greek says: "The region where we now stand was long ago called Apian in gratitude to a mortal man, a healer. For, coming from neighboring Naupaktos [a port on the northern shore of the Gulf of Corinth], Apis, healer-and-prophet, son of Apollo, cleansed this land of wild, man-destroying beasts, to which injured Earth, besmeared by the pollutions of ancient blood-deeds, had given birth. . . . For cutting out and loosening these pains irreproachable Apis is remembered in the Argive land and given recompense in prayer." Naupaktos notwithstanding, Apis is the bull-headed Egyptian god, son of Isis, who is portrayed with horns or a crescent moon on her head. The close physical correspondence between this pair and Io-Epaphos is obvious. Aeschylus surely recognized it and also the near identity of Apis' and Epaphos' names. The connection is clear in the reference here to "irreproachable Apis" and later to Epaphos "son immune to reproach" (777). Danaos seems to try to put himself into this picture when he tells his daughters that he is going to the city of Argos to muster help: "A call to arms—no, the people won't reproach its clarion" (1025).

352-62 *Strangers spin me tales . . . fleshfeasting Amazons* Aeschylus' geography here leaves Greece and sweeps through the eastern Mediterranean to "Ethiopia's borders," which in classical times meant India, and rests finally on the shores of the Black Sea, homeground of the Amazons. The imagery invests the Suppliants with lush sexuality, and they are made to seem potentially dangerous.

368-98 *A keeper of the keys to Hera's house . . . EGYPT!* This passage bristles with problems. First, it is corrupt; lines and phrases have been lost. Then, editors do not agree about who says what, who asks, who answers. There is disagreement, too, about which lines are questions. I have followed the Loeb version throughout, partly because I think that dramatic irony is well served by having the Suppliants interrogate Pelasgos rather than the other way round. That they immediately take the offensive and make Pelasgos defend himself does show a desperate cunning in their characters. They are as fierce as they look. I have also accepted the Loeb conjectures about the missing lines; such are bracketed in the translation.

Textual difficulties do not obscure what I believe is a third geography. Pelasgos has described his realm; he has speculated about the Suppliants' homeland. Here Io's line is described as producing gods and nations. The Epaphos-Apis correspondence has been mentioned. Belos can be undisguised as Baal, the golden calf, another bull god. Libya and Egypt are the eponymous founders of the lands that bear their names; Agenor can be equated with Canaan. It is almost as if the earth without Io would have been an earth without North Africa, Palestine, and the pyramids.

367 *Hera's house*   Her temple. Hera, patron goddess of Argos, presided over the sanctity of marriage. A love-affair between her priestess and her consort was sure to arouse queenly wrath.

385 *lower Nile and the city of sphinxes*   The Greek says *Canopus and Memphis*. Again I replace ancient names with words that are meant to be evocative for the reader here and now.

390 *Libya, great and fertile*   The line is not clear. It seems to say *Libya who harvests the greatest* word missing *on earth*. Though Libya now appears in imagination as an arid land where the greatest harvest is subterranean oil, it was anciently much admired for its fertile soil. Herodotos speaks of its three yearly harvests, each successively farther inland and at higher altitudes (*Histories* 4.199). I chose to emphasize fertility in the translation because of the play's general obsession with the subject and because of the vegetable image in the near line, "Had she another offshoot?" The Greek word *blastēmos*, scion or sprout or offshoot, is an urgent green word.

414-25 *Or have they violated laws . . . the burden of Zeus Suppliant's wrath*   Again, the text is not easy to interpret, and two lines are missing. I have not tried to re-imagine them. Despite corruption, the dialogue seems packed with implications. Pelasgos tries to understand the Suppliants' motive for seeking asylum. Hatred, to his good Greek logic, is too intangible a reason for behaving in a fashion that defies social expectations. Women in his world marry; love and hatred do not figure in the arrangements. He seeks a reason that he can accept: perhaps the Egyptians have performed a criminal act that would cause the Suppliants to reject and denounce them. The Suppliants, however, appeal to Pelasgos' emotions, not his reason, and they avoid giving a direct answer. Though they cite heaven's law and suggest that it overrides any manmade law, the conclusion to be drawn is that the Egyptians do indeed have valid legal claim to the women. Pelasgos' earlier hunch that these Suppliants endanger Argos receives confirmation. From his point of view their response is lunatic. But his reverence for the gods outweighs his fear that the women bring sure calamity in their train.

423 *your state's helmsmen*   The idea of the state as a ship is frequently expressed in Greek literature. And what more natural for a seafaring people?

426-517 *Son of this Ancient Ground . . . Earthly justice is yours to achieve*   The exchange between the Suppliants and Pelasgos is truly an adversary proceeding. The Greek resounds with legal terminology. The stage becomes a court of law. And it is not only the Suppliants and Pelasgos who are at odds, but two kinds of law, the unwritten code of heaven and the rules legislated by men. Try as he will, Pelasgos cannot explain to these alien, and increasingly alienating, women how firmly he is bound to respect his country's laws and its form of government. Some scholars have felt that Aeschylus, letting his pen run away with him, overstressed Argive democracy or that he was making a point we cannot now grasp. To me, however, the confrontation seems not to be imbalanced or obscure. The conflict here becomes polarized. Rationality is set against irrationality, moderation against excess. The Suppliants, whose foreignness is brought into high relief, are shown retreating from reality into fantasy.

443 *Themis*   The Suppliants cry out to the personification of the moral basis of manmade laws and customs. The invocation holds a horrible irony.

444 *Zeus Jury-Appointer*   The epithet could be translated as *Apportioner* or *Lot-Caster*. Juries were chosen by casting lots, and I have emphasized this aspect of the epithet.

453 *my private hearth*   The hearth was the heart, warm and sacred, of an ancient household.

461 *You   the people!*   The Greek says *You indeed the polis.* See note above (l. 30) on the word *polis.*

462 *pharaoh*   The Greek word is *prytanis,* which generally signifies *ruler* or *lord* and can also denote a tribal leader or a magistrate. Pharaoh, however, seems a title that would slip easily from the tongues of Egyptian refugees.

476 *His gaze*   A fatherly eye—Greek *skopos,* literally *look-out*—rests on the play. To have and to be *skopos,* to possess such an all-seeing outlook, is a gift usually reserved for deity. See notes below ll. 877-9, 946, 1046.

483-90 *If—hear me! . . . none whatever, over you* Pelasgos again indicates his suspicion that the Suppliants may be breakers of man's law. The issue of their defense, however, is moot; in this play it does not come to the test. It is perhaps easiest, here and now, to read the passage as one more attempt on Pelasgos' part to make the women see reason. Their response is again emotional.

511-12 *God Whose hands/weighing* The image of Zeus weighing or balancing scales is used directly once again in the play (1096). And Aeschylus worked two oblique changes on the picture, both in reference to the men of Argos who vote "not ambivalently" (825) and are "saviors, weighed/and found not wanting" (1297-98).

521 *eye undazed by the sea's winy rapture* The Greek speaks of an "eye not over-intoxicated." The phrase has often been understood as signifying an eye not confused in its perceptions; most translators omit any suggestion of the effects of alcohol. The Greek words, however, are not metaphoric. And the Greeks, as a sea people, surely knew about nitrogen narcosis, that rapture of the deep, which can make the fathoms-down diver feel as drunk as a toper. Pelasgos' language here and elsewhere is salted with sea-imagery.

535-64 *Be counseled and become . . . downstreaming from Zeus* These four stanzas are nothing other than a good old-fashioned curse, calling heaven's wrath upon Pelasgos and his descendants, should he thwart the Suppliants.

550 *godstones* The Greek word, *bretas*, signifies a wooden image. But because the modern mind will probably imagine the gods in terms of museum marbles, I substitute stone for wood.

571-3 *last nail driven home . . . strains toward the sea* Aeschylus' metaphor has undergone (I refuse to say suffered) a seachange. In the original it is a highly compressed nineteen syllables, a line and a half, and it is not translatable without resort to paraphrase. The gist is, "And as a ship's hull, the nails driven in, is held fast in shipyard winches, so am I held fast." In my version, nails, ship, and winches remain, but I inject the idea of a launching, of future events now set into unrecallable motion. Either way, Pelasgos means that he is gripped by the absolute necessity of making a decision he can never change.

576-7 [*in jealous charity/make good the loss*]   This is my guess. The line is griev-
ously damaged. It seems to say something about cheating and refill-
ing with plenteous cargo.

580 [*or twist the arrow in the wound*]   Again, a guess. The line is either corrupt or
interpolated. As it stands, it seems to mention grief of spirit and
agitation.

588-9 *Your animosity/repels and pulls me in*   The single verb that I have translated as *repels and pulls me in* is a verb with many shades of meaning that all involve either *go* or *come*. The line literally says, "Truly,
deeply, I much shrink-from/am-brought-into these quarrels."

593-6 *a killing night . . . for peace, for light*   No, Aeschylus' poetry does not
rhyme. And the Greek says, "I wish to be ignorant of evils rather
than wise in them, but may matters go well, though my opinion is
that they won't." But such a bald translation has no force as poetry
in English.

645-7 *of the tutelary gods/those city-guarding crocodiles that slumber/in the life-
stream of your nation*   These lines translate three words, *tōn polis-
soukhōn theōn*, which usually appear in English as *of the city-
protecting gods. Polissoukhos* (nominative form of the adjective) is,
however, a rare compound that I think must be loaded with con-
notations. *Polis*, of course, is the word signifying people-nation-
state-society. And if one reads through the alphabetized list of *polis*
compounds in the lexicon, sure enough, there is the definition, *city-
protecting*, for the double-barreled word. But, when one looks up
soukhos alone, the definition given is *crocodile*. In the mind of
Danaos the Egyptian, why should Argos' gods *not* seem to be crocodiles, as hidden and holy and dangerous as Nile's sacred beasts?

652 *Io's fathering river*   Inakhos, the Argive king who fathered Io and a river and
a river deity therefore, is the name given in the text.

660 *the firesides of gods*   The Greek says *hearths* and refers to the fires that burn
on the altars of the gods' temple-houses.

661-6 *You instructed him . . . How can it keep me safe?*   And why does Pelasgos
instruct the Suppliants to leave the safety of the shrine? Aeschylus

as playwright had a purely technical reason for moving the women from the sanctuary height to level ground or, in stage terms, from the raised stage to the orchestra. After Pelasgos makes his exit, the Suppliants sing and dance. The raised stage was not the conventional place for choral dancing. In the Greek, Pelasgos merely tells the Suppliants to descend to level ground and, though they are reluctant to abandon their refuge, he reassures them and they descend. In the translation I have added an explanation to Pelasgos' instruction so that a lone reader, not necessarily concerned with such ancient details, can imagine that the Suppliants might welcome a chance to stretch their legs after huddling in the sanctuary.

684-813 *Lord over lords . . . has completed whatever His will/conceives* At play's mid-point, in this magnificent central ode, the Suppliants act out their deepest wishes when they sing and dance the prayer-framed story of Io's torment and transfiguration. As a poet I feel that strange things are happening. In the evocation of Io, time collapses as her ancient past enters and fills the play's present moment. And in the simultaneous existence of past and present, the finite stage reaches into the universe and the mortal Suppliants glow briefly with divinity.

714 *mindbroken she runs* Yes, Aeschylus does use the present tense. It has been thought of as an historical present and is often, therefore, translated as a past. In the lines that follow I have made free with the tenses originally used because after Io here moves into the present, I prefer to keep her there as if she were actually on the stage.

721-33 *hurls her body down Asia . . . scythes grain in the fields.* A fourth geography (see also ll. 319-27, 352-62, 367-98), and I have taken great liberties with it in order to make evocative English poetry. For the Greekless here is a literal translation of the lines: "And she hurls herself through Asian lands, straight through sheepgrazing Phrygia. And she passes the town of Teuthras the Mysian, and Lydian valleys; and through the mountains of the Cilicians, of the Pamphylians, too, she rushes on to everflowing rivers and deep-rich soil and Aphrodite's grain-fertile fields."

737 *at the green oasis holy to Zeus* Io arrives in Egypt. The Greek says not *oasis* but *sacred grove* or *precinct*. I choose a word that refugees from Egypt might use.

740-43 *where quick showers strike . . . to rainsmoke*   The Greek has Typhō strik-
ing or attacking "the snowsuckled pasture." Typhō is, in one view,
the personification of a whirlwind. In Greek imaginations he was the
monstrous child of Earth and Tartarus. After he had variously attacked the Olympian gods, they fled to Egypt to avoid his assaults.
Zeus at last managed to catch him and bury him beneath Mount
Aetna, where his smoky breath still erupts. His name, in fact, signifies
smoke and smouldering. He has also been equated with the Egyptian
deity Set, who killed Osiris, the husband of Isis. And Isis, as has been
mentioned, was the crescent-horned mother of Apis. Some mytholo-
gists see her as a nature goddess and the murderer Set, therefore, as
destruction or decay in nature. I dodge all these complications and
settle for *rainsmoke* and *quick showers*. Typhō's attacks appear only
as a series of curt English k-sounds.

750-51 *and the people whose lives/the rich land sustains*   The Greek moves here
into the past tense and merely says *the people who at that time lived
in the land*. I retain the present because I feel that Io is still onstage.

768 *Zeus . . .*   This one word is all that is left of a seven-syllable line.

771 *she found rest*   Past tense in English, past tense in Greek: I think that this is
the moment at which the Suppliants release Io and let her return to
her own elder time.

789 *Danaos enters right.*   Most editors and translators see Danaos entering immediately after the Suppliants have finished singing their ode. I think
that an entrance at this point is more dramatically effective in modern terms.

794-5 *The Father/Urge of my green life*   Yes, the Greek says *patēr*, father. The
Suppliants' confusion about their father's identity begins to show.

829 SETTLERS IN OUR MOTHERLAND   The word *settlers* indicates that Danaos and
his daughters have not been granted citizenship, which carried with
it voting rights for men and certain rights of property and inherit-
ance. They are all, nevertheless, granted freedom of the *polis* and
full protection. As for *motherland*, the Greek merely says *land*. I add
the qualifier to evoke Io.

843-4 *doubly guests and kinsmen . . . double mist of blood*   Because the Suppliants are both guests and distant kinsmen of the Argive people, any

evil they might cause would have a twofold effect. The lines recall the healing work of Apis, who once cured Argos of a hideous pollution, and they also foreshadow events to come. The Suppliants will indeed stain Argive soil with blood.

861-942 Now O gods/created of God . . . written in godgiven law I have imagined this ode sung in antiphonal choruses, one of high bright voices, the other of dark-timbred voices. The strophes seem to divide themselves into two somewhat alternating groups. Some blessings are couched in positive terms: "Nation! be governed well." Others catalogue horrors that the Suppliants hope will *not* decimate the Argive people: "Never may they know the peace/that scorched earth brings." The storm gathers force. War and sickness and murder are the housegifts that the Suppliants bring to their Argive hosts.

877-9 Zeus/Avenger's eye/No battling that gaze Here again is *skopos* (see note, l. 476), the divine ability to see everything, everywhere. In these lines the god's eye, his steady gaze, becomes a bird.

890-91 Never may a plague/of men drain this nation The Greek is as ambiguous as the English. Plague may be understood as epidemic sickness or as an attack force of soldiers, *of men*. Both can drain the nation, the *polis*, of her men.

895 Ares Manmurderer Ares, too, bears epithets. Soon hereafter he is called Tearbreeder (l. 913).

907 Artemis! Hekate! Artemis, as a goddess with special interest in women's affairs, not only kept an eye on chastity and unmarried girls, but protected women in childbirth. The goddess Hekate, at Zeus' behest, guarded the well-being of children. By invoking her, the Suppliants bless not only women in labor but the infants that are struggling to be born. In light of the Suppliants' determination not to marry, the blessing is ironic.

917 Apollo of Wolves The Greek calls him *Lykeios*, an epithet that is closely related to the word for wolf, *lykos*. Apollo was thought to be both a protector of wolves that might threaten a man's enemies and a killer of wolves that attacked herds. Surely the Suppliants here call to him as one who keeps cattle safe.

936-42 *This is home earth for gods . . . written in godgiven law*   The Greek uses only the adjective *triton*, third, as I have used it. The two preceding rules are not enumerated. They are, however, plainly there in the passage. (Thank you, John Herington.)

947-53 *I see the ship./She is well marked . . . from the helm astern*   What a vivid picture Danaos creates! And here one catches sight of the notion that an inanimate thing, a ship, is somehow alive. The eyes painted on the bows possess a mysterious but very real ability to *see*.

946 *From this high holy refuge the eye gazes far*   That gazing eye is *skopē* here, a *place of look-out*. The word is perilously similar to *skopos* (see note, l. 476). Danaos does not use a pronoun to qualify the gaze but it is patently his. Nevertheless, he manages to claim a god's talent for himself. Does he confuse himself with Zeus?

969-70 NOT ONE SHALL DARE TOUCH YOU!/*No need to dread them, no need to run.*   The literal translation of the Greek is tedious: "But nothing shall come of these things; do not flee-in-fear from them. But, O but, the Greek is full of hard, short d-sounds and t-sounds. I try to reproduce them.

984 *They are a shoal of sharks*   Aeschylus does not mention *sharks* but describes Egypt's offspring as *margon*, an adjective with multiple meanings— lustful, mad, gluttonous. I have used the shark image for two reasons. First, it pictures concretely the mindless greed implied by *margon*; the Egyptians' seaborne pursuit of the Suppliants is activated by an impulse akin to the one that triggers a feeding frenzy. Then, it complements the animal images that do appear in the text soon hereafter when the Suppliants compare the Egyptians to other carnivores, *dogs* and *carrion crows*.

986 *Hulls quest, shot spears*   The Greek says *sturdy-timbered ships*, ships that are well-built. For the sake of a vivid picture in English I have made much of the fact that the Greek words for *timber* and *spear* are similar in appearance and sound, if not in etymology. I see sleek ships slicing the water with unstoppable force.

1006-7 *It is said that wolves . . ./that papyrus cannot seed the grainfields.*   These expressions are clearly proverbial. The literal reading of the second is, "Papyrus' fruit does not prevail over grain." I think that my version points up the play's emphasis on fertility without sacrificing the proverb's sense.

1016-17 *And Night/likes mothering birthpains in the skillful helmsman.* This odd expression—odd, at any rate, to us—is quite literally translated. Don't disbelieve it. The thought is that the primordial goddess Night, obscuring human vision, takes divinely malicious pleasure in spawning anxiety and fear in all men, and most especially in one who must perform his task in darkness. One might paraphrase the lines this way: The skillful helmsman, charged with securing a ship at night in a strange harbor, has his stomach tied in knots.

1020 *until the ships themselves feel snug at their moorings* Again, an indication that ships are alive and sentient. It is the *ships*, not the helmsmen, who must feel secure.

1027-98 *io io ioioioioio/O Earth . . . can steady the deathbound* This ode, like the first one that the Suppliants sing, is a lament. Thoughts of death and marriage are intertwined and sung in grieving voices. It may be of interest to note that ritual lamentation, a Greek practice with a traceable literary history spanning two and a half millennia, is not necessarily confined to the occasion of death. Emigration, exile, and marriage have also given rise to dirges. In the case of marriage there seem to be several initiating impulses. One is simply the structural similarity of Greek wedding and funeral rites. Another is symbolic similarity; the girl leaves her father's house and her childhood as truly and forever as the dead leave earth and life. In the Suppliants' song the two occasions fuse. They sing their own bridal dirge, and Death is the husband they would embrace.

1046 *A father's eye snares me* Once again, *skopos* (see note, l. 476). The Suppliants seem to say two things in one: "What my father Danaos has seen now closes in on me like a snare" and, as if a brief recognition of their wrongheadedness bursts forth, "Zeus the Father's eye holds me in a snare from which I cannot escape."

1056 *goatfoiling* The Greek says *goatless*, and the adjective describes a rockface that is too precipitous to be climbed even by agile wild goats.

1063 *murderous bed* Greek and English both carry twin readings: that the Suppliants feel that marriage will kill them and that they will kill if they are forced to marry.

1064-65 *No! first dogs shall eat . . . a godless grave*   In Greek the Suppliants say that they do not refuse to be dogs' prey and a feast for native birds. I add an interpretation that I think would have been implicitly grasped by the ancient audience. To escape marriage the Suppliants would go to the shocking extremity of forfeiting the funeral rites that the living and the dead were owed as a religious duty. And such unhallowed burial could bring pollution in its train. But the Suppliants in their desperation care for no one but themselves.

1073 *What saving channel must I cut*   Again both Greek and English hold twin readings, statement and prophecy. The Suppliants refer here to their recent flight across the sea and they also foreshadow murder-to-come, the stabbing—"cutting"—of the bridegrooms.

1081 *Look peace on me, Father*   The word *Father*, vocative in Greek, is ambiguous and can refer to Zeus or Danaos.

1087 *Egypt's get, how ugly their self-glory*   Genos gar Aigypteion, the Greek stutters hard g-sounds. Self-glory is, of course, *hybris*.

1099-1205 *No No No NO NO-O-O-O . . . You won't squeal then that you lack rule*   The text throughout has been severely damaged. Phrases have been compacted into single nonsense words; lines and passages are garbled or lost. Line order is sometimes uncertain. Nor are editors always sure about who speaks, Suppliants or Egyptian Spokesman or, in Johansen's guess, a chorus of Egyptians. The confrontation is nevertheless the most active, the most powerful scene in the play. And a translator falls back on intuition to bring into English the vigor that still resides in the corrupted Greek.

1109 *Lord on earth*   The Suppliants cry out to the absent Pelasgos. The Greek word is gaïanax, which signifies *earthlord* or *lord-of-the-land*.

1110 SPOKESMAN   The Spokesman is a herald delegated to herd the Suppliants to the ship and to bring back intelligence. I imagine him, however, as one of the sons of Egypt and have so treated him in the translation.

1110 *Sssssssssss——*   Sousthe sousthe—hurry hurry—says the Greek. I like those hissing s's.

1111-17 *So. You. Move move . . . Chopnecks, toppleheads,/move.*   Here and in his other speeches the Spokesman seems to use a broken Greek. It is the kind of speech that a foreigner unfamiliar with a language might employ.

1114 *skin stung*   Io's gadfly is evoked.

1119 *on your dunghill*   The Greek says *epamida* or *ep' amada*; the significance is utterly lost. The usual translation, based on contextual guesswork, is *to the ship*. But the Greek word is divisible into the preposition *epi* and the noun *amis*. The lexicon defines the latter as *chamber pot* and cites its seeming occurrence here as a false reading, that is—the result of a copyist's mistake or misinterpretation. How, then, can I possibly arrive at dunghill? I hope to suggest many things: the chamber pot's contents, the height on which the Suppliants take sanctuary, the dung of cattle, and the Egyptian Spokesman's utter lack of respect for Greek gods. There is, irrelevantly, an ancient proverb involving *amis*: "Don't throw grain into a chamber pot." Nor cast pearls before swine.

1120-68 *I wish/ weltering waves had . . . from that morass where your self-blindness thrives*   The Suppliants now curse the Egyptians. In this passage both of the English compounds using *self-* are translations of *hybris*. The bracketed lines are re-imaginations of jumbled, run-on words that do, for all their unintelligibility, suggest such ideas as blood and sweetness and nobility and goats.

1138 *the springflooding water*   Nile, of course.

1139 *Only there   can you trade your cattle for brides*   The Greek line says *alphesiboion hydōr*, which is usually read as *cattle-nourishing* or *cattle-producing water*. That is, water that greens pastures which in turn produce fat cattle. But again I look back to Homer, who applies the adjective *cattle-producing* to the noun for an unmarried girl. It signifies that the girl will fetch a good brideprice. I could not resist using the adjective to recall Io and her transfiguration, the divine union in which she traded her cow-form for womanhood. And I hear the Suppliants obliquely telling the Egyptians that they, the women, are not cattle who will become brides.

1140-41 *Only there   can your lifebearing blood/ arrive at full flower*   The metaphor expresses the not-uncommon archaic notion that whatever encourages growth in the natural world also mysteriously promotes human growth and maturity. As water is needed for vegetable fertility, so is it needed for human "flowering."

1144-5 [*My earth   my line/your home is mine*] The Egyptians remind the Suppliants that they, too, are Io's descendants. Their claim to Argos is equally strong.

1156 *your wanderings tombed* The Greek mentions, instead, *Sarpedon's sandy promontory-bank-tumulus.* In any case a headland on the coast of Asia Minor is indicated, for there Sarpedon, one of the sons born in Crete to Zeus and Europa, died and was buried.

1159 *Egypt's craft* I introduce a double reading—*boat/cunning*—that does not exist in the Greek, which simply says *boat.*

1165 *a crocodile* Not *soukhos* (see note, ll. 645-7) but *khampsa* is the word translated. Herodotos says the latter is the Egyptian word for crocodile (*Histories* 2.69). The usual Greek word for the beast has a familiar ring, *krokodeilos.* Aeschylus seems to use the unusual word to emphasize, once again, the Suppliants' foreignness.

1173 *Father!* Zeus or Danaos? Either and both.

1177 and 1193 *OTOTOTOI   MA GA* and *O PA   GAS PAI   ZEU* The Greek has been transliterated. In their terror the Suppliants revert to an infant babble and cry out in elemental Indo-European monosyllables that I think need no translation. *MA* and *PA*: eternally mother and father. *GAS PAI*: Earth's child. *ZEU*: vocative of Zeus. And *OTOTOTOI*: the chatter of terror.

1179 and 1191 *His snarl* and *His clutch* In both places the Greek word indicates the sound—a howl or a cry—that the Spokesman makes. I work a small change to suggest evil manifestations of breath and touch.

1194-1205 *If none of you agrees to board ship . . . you won't squeal then that you lack rule* The order of these lines is most uncertain. I have followed Johansen's arrangement.

1200 *High lord* Pelasgos.

1257 *malt-wine* The Egyptians were beer-drinkers.

1258 *You are all in the care of friends*   The Greek says, "But all of you with your
      friendly female companions in attendance." Here is the text's first
      suggestion that the Suppliants are accompanied by maidservants,
      who may have occupied the stage from play's beginning. I do not re-
      ject this possibility outright. But these ladies have not survived trans-
      lation because I think that it is too much to ask of a contemporary
      reader that he accept such a minor chorus, whose lines (1369-1404,
      if they did utter these lines at all) can be given with more here and
      now dramatic logic to others (see note below, ARGIVE WOMEN,
      l. 1369).

1264-70 *Do you wonder where you'll live . . . sequestered quietly*   The question
      of the Suppliants' lodgings, mentioned here and in lines 1332-33, has
      provoked debate. There are those who think the matter peculiarly
      overemphasized; there are others who believe that the Suppliants'
      choice had significance in the trilogy's lost plays. In Greek feeling
      the place in which a crime occurred had bearing on the crime's grav-
      ity. And where did the Suppliants commit murder? In a sacred spot,
      in the king's house, in private lodgings? No one knows. I have tried
      to translate around these problems so that a reader will not be puz-
      zled but rather hear Pelasgos trying both to talk the Suppliants
      down from sanctuary and to find his own explanation for their lack
      of response. In the lines that follow immediately the father-domi-
      nated Suppliants do give him an explanation that he can accept:
      they are waiting for Danaos in a commendably filial fashion.

1290-92 *Our father allots . . . to serve a virgin future*   The Greek, which is made
      somewhat difficult here by the loss of several preceding lines, seems
      to say, "Take your places, dear maidservants, in the way that Danaos
      assigned you as a dowry of service to each of us." Dismissing the
      problematic servants, I have again taken great liberties and reworked
      the lines to voice the Suppliants' unrealistic expectations.

1292 DANAOS *enters right with . . . a chorus of* ARGIVE WOMEN   Though I have
      sent away the maidservants, a chorus of women is called for later
      (1369-1404). Danaos' entrance seems an appropriate moment to
      bring them onstage.

1295 *red wine outpoured*   The Greek says *poured libations*. I hope to suggest not
      only libations but the red blood that the Danaids shall spill.

1299-1339 *My account of our trials . . . love your chastity more than your lives*
Perhaps I have overplayed Danaos' homily to his daughters. But the
Greek, which is usually translated as the good and gentle advice of a
devoted father, seems to me to strip Danaos of all pretense. He is
revealed as an egotistical old man full of despair at dwindling virility.
If his lusty days are over, then his daughters' days of lovemaking shall
not begin. Brackets indicate my reconstruction of two lines that are
almost unintelligible in the text; the only words that come through
clearly are *Kypris proclaims.* Kypris, the Cyprian, is one of Aphrodite's epithets.

1345-1368 *Go forth in brightness exalting . . . Out of that prize wells the river of
death* O the phallic rivers! And O the Suppliants' absolute rejection of their fertilizing flow! In the Greek, as in the translation, the
movement from praise to rejection is abrupt and takes place in mid-
strophe. Madness has pulled its snare tight.

1349 *who hallow the landloving rivers* The Greek mentions the gods who
"around-dwell the ancient stream of Erasinos." I drop the now-
unresonant name and make use of its similarity to the word *eros.*

1368 *the river of death* The Greek says, "Would that this prize come to the ones
I hate." One may also translate the last phrase as "to the stygian
ones." And another river is brought by name into the Suppliants'
ode. The river Styx—the river Hate, that is—was the black stream
across which the dead were ferried into Hades.

1369 ARGIVE WOMEN These are the women that I would have Danaos bring onstage to replace the maidservants whose thousand-line silence does
not make much here and now sense. And the lines seem to im-
ply local knowledge that foreign maidservants simply would not have
had. Johansen has assigned the verses to Danaos' honor guard of
spearmen. I cannot accept his suggestion because the words are, in
my opinion, women's words and they would not sit easily on a spear-
man's tongue.

1372 *heaven's queen* Hera.

1378 *Union* The goddess is the Greek Harmonia, daughter of Aphrodite and Ares.
She presided over all things joined, from ship's planking to strings-
and-instrument and people coupled in love.

1405-1422 *Zeus! Lord on high!* . . . *God, end and beginning of help* I have taken such liberties with strophe and antistrophe that it is only fair to give the Greekless reader a prose approximation of them. Hyphenated words indicate some of the readings possible in the Greek.

"Zeus lord, may he avert-withhold-rob me of destructive marriage to an evil man, for Zeus is the very one who with goodwill loosed Io from her miseries with his healing-triumphal hand that possessed-held her down and planted his kind force.

"And may he extend power-rule-mastery to women. I will be content with whatever is the better thing than evil, even the two-thirds share. And in accord with my prayer, may heaven's justice follow the just, with my deliverance granted by the means-devices that come from a god."

GLOSSARY

AGENOR, third-generation descendant of Io; son of Libya; brother of
Baal; when he was king of Canaan, his daughter Europa was
seduced by Zeus, who disguised himself as a bull; his son Kad-
mos founded Thebes.

AIGYPTOS, see EGYPT.

AMAZONS, a matrilineal tribe of female warriors occupying territory on
the southern shore of the Black Sea; they relegated household
tasks to men.

APHRODITE, goddess of sexual love, who rose from the seafoam near
Cyprus.

APIS, a healer and a hero to the Argive people, who honored his memory in prayers because he had cured their land of a grievous
pollution.

APOLLO, god of light and reason, excellence and order; especial patron
of athletic skill and the arts, including music and mathe-
matics.

ARES, god of war and civil strife.

ARGOS (1.) a city located on the northeasternmost peninsula of the
Peloponnese and a state claiming territory far into northwestern Greece.
(2.) the thousand-eyed watchman sent by Hera to keep Io
from accepting the attentions of Zeus.

ARTEMIS, goddess of untamed creatures and virgin wilderness, archery
and the hunt, the moon and all matters pertaining to women;
twin sister of Apollo.

BAAL, third-generation descendant of Io; son of Libya; brother of
Agenor; father of Danaos and Egypt.

DANAOS, fourth-generation descendant of Io; brother of Egypt; father
of the fifty Suppliants.

DIKE, personification of natural order and the divine laws that govern that order.

EARTH, the primal goddess Gaia, ur-grandmother of Pelasgos.

EGYPT, fourth-generation descendant of Io; brother of Danaos and uncle to the Suppliants; father of fifty sons.

EGYPTIANS, the fifty sons of Egypt and fifth-generation descendants of Io; nephews to Danaos; first cousins of the Suppliants.

EPAPHOS, son born to Zeus and named Epaphos, which signifies caress, for the manner of his conception.

HEKATE, goddess especially commissioned by Zeus to protect children.

HERA, consort of Zeus and jealous guardian, therefore, of all conjugal bonds; patron goddess of Argos.

HERMES, divine herald and messenger of the gods; guide for those who search.

IO, an Argive princess, daughter of Inakhos and priestess of Hera; her union with Zeus began the Suppliants' line.

LIBYA, granddaughter of Io and Zeus; queen of the land that bears her name; by Poseidon she became the mother of Agenor and Baal.

PELASGOS, king of the Argive people; descendant of the goddess Earth.

POSEIDON, god of ocean, earthquakes, and horses; his symbol is a three-pronged spear.

SKY, the primal god Ouranos, husband of Earth.

SUPPLIANTS, the fifty unmarried daughters of Danaos and fifth-generation descendants of Io; first cousins of the Egyptians.

THEMIS, personification of the moral basis of human customs and laws.

ZEUS, king of the gods and Hera's consort; four-times great grandfather of the Suppliants.

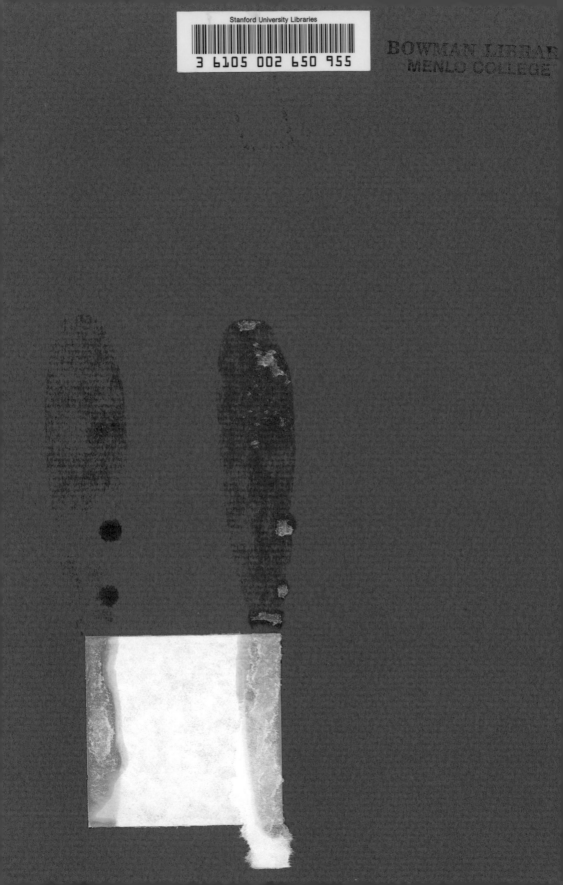